CALLING

CALLING

CALLING

A Reappraisal of Religious Life

JOSEPH J. SIKORA, S.J.

HERDER AND HERDER

1968
HERDER AND HERDER NEW YORK
232 Madison Avenue, New York 10016

Nihil obstat: Brendan W. Lawlor, Censor Librorum
Imprimatur: ✠Robert F. Joyce, Bishop of Burlington
December 20, 1967

CONTENTS

CONTENTS

CALLING

I.

IS VOCATION
A VIABLE CONCEPT?

EVERY man is called by God to abandon the road which by nature he is inclined to take, and to enter upon the road which leads to eternal divine life. Man's first response to this call of God—a response that can be made only with the help of divine grace—is faith. Faith is believing acceptance that God has in fact spoken to men in history, and that he still does speak to every man. It is to believe that God offers to us the saving good, a higher life with himself that even now begins to raise us above our natural fragility and our innate moral ambivalence and weakness, though its fullness and consummation must await our natural death.

We must, of course, begin by simply accepting God's word, and all that it says. But such an acceptance is already and simultaneously, and even first in the order of logical priority, a trust in and commitment to the Person who speaks to us. The revelation of God does not call for acceptance based on a merely reasoned-out conviction of his truthfulness that would regard him as some kind of infallible manipulator. This revelation is a call to a new life, which has norms all its own, and it requires that the hearer trust God as personally speaking the truth to him. We must be quite prepared—it is in fact prerequisite—to rely upon God's own light rather than our own. It is not a natural confidence in our ability to find an infallible source of truth, but rather a supernaturally inspired confidence in God's own light, that helps us to make such a radical reversal in our perspective. We simply could not escape from and transcend the limitation of natural intellect without a supernatural light that enables us to accept a supernatural revelation on God's terms rather than on our own.

Such an understanding of the Christian vocation, whether it be explicitly Christian or only anonymously so, enables us to see why Abraham is the father of all believers. God calls us to go into another land, to a new supernatural domain, where mere human customs and laws are no longer the determining norms. This new land is the kingdom of God, and to get there we must grow in communion with God, we must make our way there with the light of divine grace.

Those who would follow the call of God must therefore leave themselves and abandon their old ways. But this is a painful process; growth in the Christian life is a slow and gradual thing, and it is necessary for the wayfarer continually to struggle against the tendency to follow only his natural instincts and only natural laws. This dynamic struggle—patterned on the passion, death, and resurrection of the Lord—is the most essential aspect of our suffering growth in the grace of Christ.

Yet the providence and love of God guide each of us towards himself, so that we can say with confidence that all things work together unto good for them that love God. Thus we can speak of individual vocations, for God's providence and love lead men along various ways to the kingdom; every man has his unique vocation to respond to the particular call of God to him, as this call comes to him in the many circumstances of his life.

Within the visible Church four generic "vocations" can be distinguished, in accordance with the choice of functions that members of the mystical body of Christ can assume. Three of these have long been recognized: the priesthood, married life, and the religious life; the fourth has been acknowledged only in more recent years, that of the single life dedicated to God. Of course, when we distinguish four such "vocations" within the Church, we are using the term *vocation* in a quite specialized sense. We could further specialize the term by speaking of So-and-so's vocation to be married to this woman and to no other, or to a sister's vocation in this congregation and not that.

But we must exercise caution in speaking of "vocation" in such a manner, as though it automatically implied logical classification. Such a manner of speaking might easily lead us to regard "vocation" as only a category by means of which we could classify the people of God according to their role in the Church. And in this way the uniquely personal character of every vocation would be entirely disregarded. It would be to view from the perspective of a system rather than from the individual perspectives of unique personalities. It would be to negate the sense of high drama, the profound "moment of truth," that is at the heart of every call from God and every human response to it. It is not idle poesying to say that the angels and blessed never cease to speak of what we mortals do.

Thus, even when we speak of the nature of religious vocation in general, we must preserve the sense of it being a uniquely personal matter between real human people and a very loving God.

The questions that are being asked today concerning the

11

value of the religious state in the Church are not without serious provocation. There was and is still a widespread conviction among many of the laity that the heights of Christian holiness could not be reached by one who lived in the world and who did not enter into the vowed religious life. It was generally felt that either the priesthood or the religious life were the proper places to pursue the lofty goal of greater union with God in love.

Now Vatican II has affirmed in a most clear manner that God has called the whole people of God to loving union with himself —even to the very heights of sanctity. But if this is so, then God has given the means, the grace, to attain that goal. The perplexing question which naturally results is: Why then should anyone "leave the world" in order to follow the way of the evangelical counsels in religious life?

The issue is further complicated by the fact that one of the requirements of any apostolate in the modern world is marked adaptability in the face of change—yet religious communities have an inherent stability (this is indeed one of the reasons for their existence in the first place). Within religious communities there is a quite obvious tendency not readily to change ways of life and methods of work. In this respect, they appear to be rather outmoded within modern culture, and not places where one would expect to find imaginative and creative apostolates.

In addition, it is all too easy to point to many concrete deficiencies in the functioning of the religious communities in the modern world, to so many inadequacies in their attitudes towards the values of religious life. There is even confusion among the religious communities on the practice of the three basic vows of poverty, chastity, and obedience. In an age that accords primary respect for the unique values of the human person—freedom,

fulfillment of potential, responsibility, initiative, and so forth—
there is much in religious life that gives grounds for suspicion
that these values are not fully taken into account. Further, how
are such things as the cross, mortification, humility, and abnegation to be understood within the modern cultural context? Is it
even possible to justify such religious values in our contemporary
culture, or with the values of the human person? If it is not,
then there is no good reason for the Church to continue to support and encourage the practice of the religious life.

It would do no good, of course, to consider these matters simply
at the level of the liberal-conservative conflict which so much
troubles the life of the Church today, for the question goes much
deeper than what is convention or non-convention. We must
consider man in a philosophical and theological way, and attempt
to think through in a "metaphysical" way the ground for religious and human values, and try to see them in full perspective.
We must try to see if perhaps some statements on and descrip-
tions of the religious values of the religious life do not need, after
all, a good deal of amplification and deepening in order that
traditional understanding of them can be "developed"—in a
manner analogous to the development of dogma itself. It might
well be that such a developed understanding of the primary
values of religious life in the light of contemporary understanding of man and his relations to the world and God would even
give grounds for a more perfect living of the Christian life in
the religious state, and consequently would provide a thoroughly
grounded reaffirmation of the value and dignity of the religious
state.

While there are many problems concerning the religious life
in the modern world, we propose to consider here only the

four major general objections to the general idea of a religious life in community under vows in the Church today. Specific problems relating to particular values of religious life—such as poverty, chastity, obedience, love for the cross of Christ, mortification, and humility—will be taken up later in the book.

The first objection has already been suggested. Religious life is described as a "state of perfection" in which each person is obliged—because he has freely taken on this obligation—to strive for Christian perfection. But in light of the Council's affirmation that every Christian is called to live a life of Christian perfection, how can we speak of a particular "state of perfection"?

Another objection, also briefly touched upon, is that the religious life seems to be itself a serious impediment to apostolic efficiency. The rather slow adaptation of religious communities to changing conditions, the more or less conservative attitudes on the part of those in authority in most communities, the resulting discontent felt among the more progressive members of the communities, —all of these considerations lead to the popular opinion that truly involved and committed apostolic action within religious communities is impossible on a full-time, full-spirited basis. The conclusion is that a religious community simply cannot be an efficacious means for the exercise of the apostolate.

The third objection is that religious life in many communities often appears to be as much an inhibition as a help to spiritual growth. We might recall that St. Teresa of Avila once said that anyone seriously attempting to seek God and enter into deep communion with him and serve him perfectly would find his worst enemies in his fellow religious. Obviously, the present problem is not a new one.

A final difficulty, one that is frequently pointed out, is that the religious life prevents most of those who live it from ever reaching that degree of human development, of human maturity and growth to the fullness of one's potentialities, that can be reached elsewhere. This difficulty touches upon some very profound theological matters concerning the complex relationship between natural human life and the supernatural life of divine grace in us.

Without willingness and even readiness to face these objections honestly, there can be no development of our understanding of the religious life. The idea of the religious life must grow, just as other ideas must grow in keeping with the development of human culture.

There is no question, of course, of arbitrarily giving up the idea of religious life in the Church, or of discarding all of the ideals of the religious life which were formulated in earlier centuries. Yet it is possible that with the reformulation of the ideal, which has already slowly begun, the memberships of the communities will decline sharply. Still, it is also possible that religious communities will retain their important place in the life of the Church. Vatican II has strongly reaffirmed the importance of the religious life in its *Decree on the Appropriate Renewal of the Religious Life.* For religious communities, besides being environments where those called by God may more easily live the life of the evangelical counsels in a more perfect manner, are also in the name of the Church a living testimony to and an anticipation of the eschatological state of man with God. They are a clear indication on earth of the real finality and the real tendency of the life of grace.

However, such affirmations of the desirability of the religious life are not affirmations of its absolute need—the Church could survive, though to its great loss, without religious communities. Nor are these affirmations meant to be answers to the objections which we have listed above. It is not enough simply to carry on. There can be reaffirmation of the value of the religious life, but there must also be a re-evaluation of its functioning in the modern world, specifically in relation to its primary values and the three fundamental counsels of poverty, chastity, and obedience.

God calls all of us to the Christian vocation. He also calls some individuals to a more intimate communion with himself and to a loving service in work for the coming of his kingdom on earth as the anticipation of its fullness in heaven. But even though this special call has in times past, and in the present, been a call to many to enter and to live in religious communities of one kind or another in the Church, still the difficulties we have raised do seem to be reason for some hesitation today. Many who would generously respond to God's call can be genuinely uncertain about whether he actually calls them to life in a religious community.

Since the call of God is always a call to an individual person in his unique situation, there is no point here in making general remarks about the advisability of entering into a religious community. But it is possibe to clarify the meaning of this religious state of life, and to make some reply to the four general objections enumerated earlier. It is true that many particular problems will remain unresolved; but if the supernatural call of God to man is always a call like that to Abraham, into an unknown way, and even into the desert, it is possible for a person to respond to this call, if not with a clear knowledge of all of the obstacles to be met and surmounted, then at least with confidence that God takes care of those whom he loves and that he will

16

give the necessary light, and the supernatural means, to follow the call. No one should expect the religious life to be a "high road to heaven," where all is light. In following Christ, we must all take up our cross—this is more than ever true of any serious attempt to live the religious life of the evangelical counsels. And we must always prepare ourselves to suffer from the inadequacy of others, of customs, of institutions, of rules and regulations, as well as of ourselves—as Christ prepared himself.

The religious state, as we have noted, is called a "state of perfection" in the Church. This is well enough understood to mean not a state for those only who are already perfect in Christian love, but rather a state for those who are striving to attain a high degree of love and communion with God and service of him and their fellow men. Yet even this qualification seems now to be quite insufficient. After all, are not all Christians to seek for this degree of perfection? Is there not an implicit denial of this possibility for other Christians in the very existence of the religious state?

What is more advantageous about the religious state in the pursuit of holiness is that the life of the evangelical counsels (not just according to the letter of the vows as canonical obligations, but rather according to the profound orientations which they really signify and aid) of itself offers not just special help for reaching more intimate friendship with God, but even tends beyond what is ordinarily called friendship to a "mystical" love of God in which God becomes absolutely one's All.

The giving of self to God in such a "mystical" love is far more profound, far more complete, than that self-giving that is of the nature of truly sincere and successful marriage. In the religious life there is an unqualified following of God, wherever

17

he may lead, even into a desert darkness. What else could be the object of throwing off every chance of gaining any material possessions for oneself, of renouncing the joy of sexual communion, of trusting oneself to the providence of God in the renouncing of free choices in favor of the direction of a religious superior? Such emptying can only be intelligible in the light of a much greater fullness to come. Whatever is to be said of the ontology of infused contemplation in regard to mystical life, we must insist on the intrinsic tendency of the supernaturally inspired life of the evangelical counsels towards a profound and vitally dominant fruitive affective communion with God and with Christ, a communion that must properly be called "mystical."

The religious state in the Church is one in which this life of the evangelical counsels is lived, ordinarily in community with others, according to a given manner of life that is definitively accepted through the taking of religious vows that are publicly accepted by the Church. Insofar as it really does mean and call for a constant tendency towards God as one's All, as Everything, the religious state ought to be recognized as a state of tending towards the perfection of Christian life. This is the meaning of the assertion that the religious state is a state of perfection.

The place of religious communities in the Church is authoritatively recognized by the Church. The religious vows to God are even incarnated in the structure of the Church through the visibility of religious "profession." Thus the various religious institutes are approved, publicly recognized ways of devoting oneself wholly to God in the visible Church.

Yet we must keep in mind that the professed religious is not acting "on his own." God is the one who first moved his heart, who guided him into his entry into some religious group. Further, this guidance continues within the structures, authoritative regulations, and circumstances of that particular community in the visible Church. The professed religious can believe that this is so—that it is truly the voice of God which he encounters and hears in the community—because of the relation of this community to the hierarchical structure of the visible Church. Only if God speaks through the authority that constitutes a religious institute in the Church can the religious have reasonable assurance that God also speaks in and through his particular community. Once this authoritative approval is seen as coming ultimately from God, then the religious can view his community as a place where he can hear and follow the call of God.

It should be noted, of course, that the mere existence of such places where one can hear and follow the call of God under more ideal conditions does not entail any obligation upon anyone to enter one of them. There are many ways to God; each vocation, as we have stressed, is *sui generis*. Yet it is possible that some people could find themselves in such an attitude and situation that their entry into a given religious community, or the religious community in general, becomes really required of them if they are to be loyal to the life of grace that is in them. For such persons, to refuse to enter the religious life at this point would be also to refuse to follow the light given to them—it would be a spurning of the call of God. Still, there is no command for any man to live the life of the evangelical counsels—which is why they are called counsels and not commands. It is the spirit of the counsels which underlies the fundamental dynamism of the whole life of grace.

The important question, then, is: Who will profit, who will succeed, with the help of God, in living the life of the evangelical counsels, even in religious community life? Most men and women would find such a life physically or psychologically impossible. Those who are not suited for the religious life could soon begin to suffer from severe neurosis. On the other hand, there are other men and women who find the religious life all too compatible, as an environment which gratifies weaknesses which they must rise above in order to live a fully Christian life—homosexuality, sexual immaturity, fear of responsibility, ultradependency, masochistic inclinations, a desire for a leisurely life that leaves one free of ordinary cares. Such persons have to be firmly discouraged from any attempt to enter the religious life so long as they seek to submit to any of these weaknesses.

Frequently enough, however, there is neither clear and unmistakable evidence of a divine call, nor clear and unmistakable reason for the exclusion of this possibility. The divine call here is more like an invitation, in the ordinary sense, in that the way appears open as a real personal possibility, at least as a chance that might reasonably be taken, as a risk that is well worth being run. If along with the requisite physical, mental, moral, and spiritual qualities there is the right intention to join the religious life in a given community—and if there is receptiveness on the part of the community—then surely there is a divine vocation. Such a vocation may not be so dramatic as the call to Abraham or Paul, but it demands the same kind of trust and following in faith. It is the same call to live for God alone, to set out on a way of unlimited response of love and service—without any clear idea of just what demands God will make of us. The person who is called and chosen by God is asked to involve himself without reserve in God's work among men.

There is no occasion here, of course, for spiritual snobbery. God's free election is behind every call, and entry into the life of the counsels in a religious community—a "state of perfection"—is no guarantee that one will grow in the enthusiasm with which he may have started out. The "state of perfection" is in itself only a tremendous opportunity; the degree of our devotion to God's work in the world depends upon his grace but also upon the generosity (itself not without grace) of our response. Thus the acceptance of a religious vocation is a most serious risk; to whom much is given, from him much also is expected.

The second objection against religious life in the Church is that it seems seriously to impede real apostolic efficiency. Needless to say, every form of this objection cannot be refuted—there are some types of apostolic activity that demand complete freedom, such as politics. There are also certain kinds of personalities which require almost absolute freedom of movement, and such persons ought not to enter religious communities—or ought not to stay.

However, taking for granted the definite possibility that the structures of religious communities can be made a good deal more flexible both in theory and in practice, the value of organized work over isolated effort in many spheres is obvious enough. It is not necessary, moreover, that all religious communities be well adapted to most kinds of organized work; some communities are better adapted to one work, some to another; some to many, some to few. Some communities are more adaptable than others in allowing room for individual work.

But there are no serious grounds for saying, in light of the vast amount of apostolic work undertaken by the religious communities in the Church, that these communities are no longer effective in the apostolate. Specific criticisms are often justified, regarding specific areas of the apostolate, specific tasks, rather than specific communities.

This is not to deny that there are no ways to improve—and often greatly to improve—the functioning of religious communities in their apostolic work. But we can hardly opt for tearing down the organization altogether so long as the needs of the Church for apostolic works of every kind continue. There is no reasonable basis for an all-or-nothing brand of criticism which represents as the only two alternatives either revolutionary reform or suppression. Renewal is a middle course—and also the most difficult course. Religious communities must be made as liveable as possible, by being developed in their traditions and outlooks in the light of recent cultural growth and the progress of theological thought. Patching up here, making a suggestion there, all the while seeking the depth of profound communion with God that grace makes it possible to attain—such is the way, however slow and undramatic, of renewal.

Let us now consider the objection that structured community life is today as much an inhibition against as a help towards spiritual growth. The objection is certainly valid as it relates to some individuals; and in fact, the religious life perhaps represents serious dangers to everyone. Any human organization—not only religious communities, but also the armed forces, or civil service, or a large industrial enterprise—is dangerous for the human spirit, and must be learned about and prepared for. It is all too easy to be taken in by the "system," to allow oneself to be passively moved rather than actively to exercise one's human freedom. But this is a common danger also to all human life in society. A true and enduring interior freedom of spirit is achieved only after a conquest of one's tendencies towards nonresponsibility and laxity of spirit and creativity.

It is paradoxical that the very effort to achieve some kind of stability in following God's call wherever it may lead, by taking the religious vows of poverty, chastity, and obedience, can lead to a rather routine existence that numbs one's sensitivity to the divine call. Constant struggle is required to preserve an attitude of real openness towards hearing and following the immediate call of God. A community that encourages or at least does not oppugn passive acquiescence as opposed to active concern, creative initiative, and responsible criticism is obviously working against its spiritual vitality and its apostolic effectiveness.

Generally, however, the "system" of the religious community does tend to support the quest for deeper communion with God and greater dedication to his work in the world more than do many other human milieus. Or at least it does so for those who are in fact well-suited to such a mode of life for the reasons spoken of earlier. This is not to deny the fact that *every* human organization—with its necessary component of human mediocrity —is also an impediment to individual growth. The observation of St. Teresa of Avila concerning the difficulty that comes from one's fellow religious for anyone who sincerely seeks to give an unlimited response, with the help of grace, to the call of grace, is not so much a sharp criticism of religious communities as a simple statement of the facts of human life in this world. The religious community has its advantages, as we have pointed out; but it is still only a dwelling place of *men* who may have aspirations inspired by grace and also a share in human mediocrity. It is well to dispel any illusions to the contrary in new

23

candidates as soon as possible, in the interest of avoiding a great deal of suffering later on. It ought always to be emphasized that no religious community can constitute some ideal order of persons and things in this world, but that nevertheless religious life does offer both Christian ideals and a manner of pursuing them that do indeed constitute a "better way."

Such a "better way," in a more favorable milieu, is not a matter of small importance. The basic option of supernatural charity, which is the heart of our supernatural life with God, is both in itself and in its degree of intensity quite independent of the milieu in which it is made. Saints may be found in the most un-likely of places. But we cannot fail to recognize that some milieus are more favorable to growth in supernatural life, and even to perseverance in it, than are others. The articulation in detail of this basic option in particular acts and in the formula-tion of belief and of prayer may be far easier in one milieu than in another. Religious life in religious communities tends to favor these aspirations in a special way.

Even here there is wide variety among religious communities themselves. Differing spiritualities tend to favor different articula-tions—different in their general characteristics—of the one same loving relationship of man with God. Different temperaments in different national groups have their own influence in these mat-ters. But by and large, the very nature of religious community life as a rule tends to help one to resist the ordinary human pull towards pride and sensuality. If there are dangers to growth in real interior freedom of spirit and to spiritual growth in general, such dangers are not lacking elsewhere. At least in religious life there is usually more ample opportunity to be conscious of such dangers and to take necessary preventive means against them.

This is not reason for complacency; the need for renewal is obvious enough, and the call for renewal has been sounded by the ecumenical council. But there is reason to maintain that religious life, with and despite its deficiencies, still can and does lead many men and women to spiritual growth and even to most profound communion with God and with Christ.

Finally, we come to the fourth objection against the desirability of religious life today: that a full human life is impossible in religious community life. Such an objection could be made from several points of view. One would be the continual subordination of personal fulfillment to the needs of the group that is the religious community and to the demands of the apostolic work in which the community is engaged. Another is the rather limited circle of companions with which one must spend most of his life in such a religious community. There is also the necessary loss of a large part of ordinary human experience that must go along with entry into any such religious community at a relatively early age. Similarly, the tendency of a number of communities—though fewer every year—to educate their student-religious in a rather closed "seminary" environment could not help but deprive many of these students of opportunities for coming to a truly broad perspective and openness to all the truth in widely varying viewpoints.

In our opinion the first and last of these objections present the most serious problems for religious communities today. For this reason we shall devote much attention to them elsewhere and simply recognize here that they do imply in fact some definite limitations upon the natural human development of many members of religious communities. But it would be somewhat unfair to these communities not to note that these problems are not peculiar to religious communities, but are endemic to most large systematized groups, such as military service.

Regarding the second and third objections concerning the lack of opportunity for full human development in such a religious community, it must be recognized that the loss of a large amount of ordinary human experience, at least for those who enter religious life at an early age, is in fact a serious matter. It is quite necessary to compensate for this experience in the education of such persons. This is perhaps the most important reason for some manner of escape from, or at least supplement to, the ordinarily rather closed environment of education for religious. University life and apostolic activity of some kind that means frequent and broad human contact with outsiders are the most obvious remedies for this situation. Through such means it may be hoped that the young religious will come to adult prudence, to a healthy and balanced view about the good and the evil in men and in human affairs, and so to a moderate outlook that will avoid the extremes of naïve optimism or pessimism about the human situation.

Such means also are a way of relieving the difficulty raised for the religious by his living with a small group of companions perhaps for the rest of his life. This difficulty is not so real for religious communities dedicated to the work of some active apostolate in the world, but even in such cases, group life does present some limitations. If companionships outside the community would be enriching from a cultural or even a spiritual standpoint, then they ought to be encouraged, if at all possible— perhaps circumstances may render outside friendships unfeasible. But again, such a problem is not peculiar to the religious community; it is common to human social groups in general, and it is not at all easy to solve.

The fundamental answer to such problems that are at least for the time being apparently unresolvable is still quiet acceptance. It is divine providence which has led the religious into his circumstances. It may well be that the whole value of his situation is precisely in the manner of his response. What do such problems matter if through them he comes to a new degree of supernaturally inspired sacrificial love in union with Christ?

We do not intend by the tone of our answers to imply that nothing is wrong or in need of great improvement in the ordinary living of religious communities in the Church today. Religious life has undergone and must yet again undergo structural change and a deepening and development even of its very ideals. The cultural development of man can only be expected to lead to such changes in the appreciation of and attitude towards religious life. There is need not only to return to historical sources and to the ways of doing things in religious life of many centuries ago; rather, there is even greater need to re-examine religious ideals in the light of human cultural change, in the light of growth in human self-understanding, in the light of the progress of theological thought concerning man, his relation to the world, and his relation to God.

If all this is true then the rebuttal of some conservative spirits that certain rules and customs and so on have been "good enough for five hundred years" is quite irrelevant to the issues of today. This is no real answer to the crisis caused by real cultural change, but simply a refusal to face the problems. If we are seriously to consider improvements and developments, and to make the effort to bring them about, first it is necessary to love what we criticize. That is why we had first to make a firm defense of the religious vocation before embarking upon a critique of many of the values and ways of doing things in religious communities. Defects there may be, critiques and renewal may be quite necessary; but religious life in the Church is no hopelessly outmoded cultural form. The essential still continues today, as it has for centuries—God still calls men and women to live with him and to love and serve him alone above all else. It will still go on tomorrow, and the day after. All we can hope for is that we can contribute something in this age of renewal towards the greater perfection and success of communities that must still have at every time a certain measure of human mediocrity and failure about them. Those who would look for something more might also be unable to understand our Lord's choice of companions long ago.

II.

THE IMITATION OF CHRIST
AND THE LOVE OF THE CROSS

The notion of the imitation of Christ, and consequently the love
of and desire to share his cross, is at the heart of Christian
spirituality. It is, therefore, also fundamental in the understanding of the religious life of the evangelical counsels; and yet, if
today we can see some tendency to "play down," or even to set
aside, the ideal of suffering with Christ, this is certainly not
something new. The observation of Thomas à Kempis in Book
II, Chapter 11, of *The Imitation of Christ,* that "Few love the
cross of Jesus," is perennially true.

Although the enthusiasm of some disciples of Teilhard de
Chardin should not be confused with his own thought, nevertheless for some of these disciples the idea of simple acceptance of a
great deal of suffering is rather hard to reconcile with the conviction that the human race is really tending towards some kind
of ultimate unity and perfection even within history that will
indeed be accomplished without doubt. For them, suffering and
the cross are not so much the very substance of grace and of our
salvation as rather only an unfortunate necessity—to be avoided

29

if at all possible—of the moment at which we stand and in which we are moving in the upward evolutionary thrust. For them, the tension between human nature and the demands of the life of grace has been minimized, so that "graced" nature appears as something natural and only to be expected. Struggle there must still be—but this struggle is directed much more at overcoming the obstacles to a "utopia" here below than at growth in Christian life through the traditional ascetical means of personal prayer, mortification, and so on. There is even a radical reversal of perspective so that visible efficacy in the world is set far above the invisible efficacy in the economy of grace that goes along with grace-inspired endurance of visible failure. One wishes to imitate Christ bringing messianic blessings even in the temporal domain, but one pays less attention to the transcendence of his kingdom that is "not of this world."

Such a view as this of Christian life is itself a reaction, though a perverse one, to a previous emphasis upon the transcendence of the life of grace—an emphasis that tended to draw Christians away from involvement with the concerns of the temporal world so far as possible. There is, after all, a common temporal task for all men to make this world of ours more liveable, more fitting, for the sons of God who must pass through it. The values of this world are genuine values that call for respect and cultivation, even devotion. They are values created by God, values that are even conditions for the fullest flourishing of the divine life in man, for the fullest freedom of the human response to grace, certainly values to be assimilated into the work of building the temporal dwelling place of the city of God and of the mystical body of Christ.

Reflection on such a Christian love of the world reveals that

30

many serious difficulties still do underlie such a "positive" attitude towards the world. Much of Christian ascetical rhetoric is at least unfriendly towards this kind of attitude. One might well wonder how the imitation of Christ would be realized by men who strive to enter, not less, but more and more into the concerns of the world. And how could such men reconcile a fundamental love of and desire for the cross with total commitment to the reduction and even the elimination of so many of the evils that trouble mankind? We could raise a whole series of more specific difficulties arising both from the very nature of the human situation and from the problem of understanding just how one is after all to imitate Christ.

We have come to understand that there are indeed alternatives to the simple acceptance of suffering, that it is even possible to do away with a very large part of human suffering. If Christian faith tells us that physical suffering can be used as a valuable means for the salvation of ourselves and of the world, at the same time human reason tells us that this same suffering is in itself an evil, something to be avoided if possible, and indeed something that can be steadily lessened through the advance of technology and medicine and other areas of human knowledge and practice. Man is no longer merely at the mercy of the forces of nature, and he becomes more and more their master in the course of history. He can no longer merely submit with resignation to the necessities of nature; rather he must exert his forces so that what once was inevitable is no longer inevitable. We have a real hope of banishing from the earth most, if not all, of the illnesses that trouble us—and some even speak of indefinitely prolonging life itself.

Moreover, we feel that it is only fitting for man so to dominate

31

the forces of nature, entirely in keeping with his personal dignity, intelligence, and freedom. It is beneath the dignity of man to allow himself to fall prey to these forces without a struggle. This is all the truer when there is question, not of the blind forces of nature, but of the pressures of human society. We believe that the innate dignity of the human person calls for a continuing struggle for more and more genuine freedom for every man on earth to grow without limit in his personal life— and that the whole of organized society exists precisely in order to provide the greatest possible opportunity for such growth. Thus we owe it to ourselves and to all men to fight for such freedom, and not to submit to the encroachments of unjust authority and authoritarianism.

But such a view of human life makes it seem quite unintelligible to submit willingly to avoidable "crosses." After all, this would be to deny the very dynamism of human nature and personality towards ever greater fullness of consciousness and of all the goods of human life. In such a light, what possible sense could there be in any injunction to seek the harder way? The absurdity of such a course would seem evident even to those people with the most profoundly Christian appreciation of the personal dignity and worth of every man.

If love of the cross seems to be something as outmoded as chivalry to many moderns, the same must also be said for the ideal of the imitation of Christ in general. Clearly, it would be a serious misunderstanding to interpret the imitation of Christ as referring to the external details of his life on earth. We understand that what was done in another time, in another place, in other circumstances, in another culture, need not be an exact and adequate norm for what we must do today. But even a concept of the imitation of Christ as an imitation of his interior disposition of spirit presents a serious difficulty. We must ask ourselves how much we can really understand of the interior dispositions of Christ, whether we have any real hope of actually comprehending his reasons for embracing his particular pattern of life and for his acceptance of the cross. Would it not be possible for us to read into his actions some meaning of our own, superimposing upon his own culturally conditioned action something of our own culturally conditioned understanding? But then the imitation of Christ is a far more problematic matter than we might at first think.

Would it be reasonable to think of Christ, as true a man as any of us, enacting some kind of performance for our benefit and not rather as being deeply involved in a personal drama that was not all written in advance? If his manner of life and thought is some kind of norm for us, must it not first have been his own authentic response as man-God in unique situations totally different from our own? Do we not also have a like authenticity of our own? How then can we look to Christ as to some kind of exterior pattern for our life, without primary attention to the question of our own authenticity, of simply being ourselves. Would the imitation of Christ mean that we are to strike some kind of Christian "pose" before the world, regardless of our own inner dispositions? How could we really come to any personal and authentic love of Christ if we were not first determined to be fully ourselves?

With such considerations as the above, we must also ask what value there really is in a life of total sacrifice in the pattern of Christ, in "following" him on the way of the cross. If his sacrificial way of life had a quite definite and intelligible purpose, how can we guarantee that the same would be true in our own lives? Christ carried out the will of the Father, but how can we be certain that this will of the Father is likewise his will even for us in our twentieth-century world, for us with our "advanced" understanding of the real dignity of the human person, against whom every undeserved cross might seem a real offense and a real evil that should be eliminated so far as possible? But then insults, humiliations, and contempt cannot reasonably be objects of desire—as the old ascetical rhetoric would have it. We must look for progress in love and communion with God and man, and not for occasions in which our person can be subjected to unjust and degrading treatment from other men.

Yet most of us realize out of Christian common sense that the cross is part of Christian life, that the old ascetical rhetoric, however full of clichés, is also profoundly true. If the time has come when many will no longer listen to sound doctrine, it remains Christian doctrine nevertheless. But it is well now to go behind such formulas as "Christ suffered, and so must I, because I love him and want to be like him," and "I want to be poor with Christ poor, humiliated with Christ humiliated," and so forth. To an earlier age of Christian spirituality, perhaps less reflective, such formulas were self-explanatory, or seemed to be so, responding to the fundamental dynamism of Christian grace in men. But we require a more articulate understanding. We are too conscious of our worth as persons, and too conscious of the possibilities for psychological self-deception that lurk behind obscurity of understanding. We are too aware of the extent to which conduct, Christ's and our own, is necessarily conditioned by all manner of subjective purposes and objective circumstances. For such reasons we would wish a clearer understanding of the exact meaning of "imitation of Christ" and "love of his cross."

What we need is to see how the life and suffering of Christ is really an echo or resonance of a truly universal human condition —so that anyone as truly man as he but also acting under as truly divine a light and grace (and all the more so a man-God come to share our condition to lead us to God) would find it most appropriate to assume this kind of life in order to fit in every respect the real condition of man. Perhaps there is even a metaphysical basis for such an exemplar, a basis in the very structure of human existence in the face of the actual supernatural order and of the concrete grace of God that we are offered, indeed in the very notion of a fully free but grace-inspired transcendence by man of his "essential" human weakness, misery, and fallenness, in a higher life with God. Perhaps such an exemplar is at least required because of the kind of grace that most befits such a human condition. In any event, this exemplar must at least "befit" the kind of grace that we are in fact offered.

Such a metaphysics of the cross and of the incarnation is not unthinkable even though the incarnation and its manner are ultimately due to the radically free decision of God. This metaphysical analysis would not end in demonstrating that God *absolutely* had to act in this way and in no other (thus compromising the divine freedom), but rather in showing how our redemption through Christ in fact really does so befit the human condition that the imitation of Christ, and even the love of his cross, do indeed flow "naturally" from the structure of the concrete supernatural life that has actually been bestowed upon us in virtue of the sacrifice of Christ. This kind of understanding should also illuminate in greater detail the pattern that such imitation of Christ and love of the cross should actually take in our lives, and consequently enable us to give a more precise response to the difficulties raised above.

The grace of Christ, which has been in fact the grace offered to every man since the fall of Adam, has been God's own response to the condition in which the fall left man. As a result of the fall of Adam, man remained destined to a higher supernatural life with God but lacked in himself either the means or any kind of title to the means to live such a supernatural life and so to merit eternal communion with God. From an earlier, unfallen state in which he was somehow free from physical death and suffering, and constituted without any pain or struggle in a state of enduring friendship with God, man lapsed into the condition in which we still find him today—prey to all manner of evil, morally weak, inevitably subject even to physical death. The grace of Christ does not simply emancipate us from this state of fallenness. Even while it restores us to friendship with God, nevertheless this is a friendship that demands continual moral struggle, suffering, and sacrifice. Indeed, this friendship demands a love for God that is stronger than death, essentially sacrificial insofar as it requires willing acceptance of the pains and troubles of our mortal existence even up to the ultimate surrender of everything in death.

It is only a matter of observation that the actual redemptive plan of God through the grace of Christ does not in any way destroy a fundamental continuity between our fallen state and our redeemed state. Neither baptism nor penance work any marvellous effects within the field of ordinary experience itself, as a rule. It would certainly have been possible for God to have made an evident discontinuity here, perhaps to constitute a new human race in a new condition—not sons of Adam in any true sense of the term at all. But such a manifestation of divine power, analogous to that shown in the first creation of all things, is in a way inferior to the course that he has actually chosen. Instead, God shows both a greater power and a greater mercy by finding a way in Christ to lead and to draw men from the depths of their fallenness even to a new height of love that would have been impossible in the first economy of salvation.

For Christ has revealed to us a new mode of divine love for us and a new manner of response to the advances of God. Before the fall, man's supernatural love of God in virtue of the grace of Adam was already more than a mere love of friendship. Already it was a mystical love of God, but a mystical love without tears— in a manner effortless for man. Such a love, in its depths, already implied a readiness even to sacrifice; but this readiness would not have to face the ultimate test of the cross. But after the fall of Adam, the grace of Christ flows from God's redemptive, sacrificial, and self-immolating love manifested in Christ's own life and sacrifice; and this same grace of Christ tends towards, calls each of us to, a response in the same pattern of sacrifice and immolation through which we can ourselves cooperate in furthering the redemptive work of Christ and his grace. This Christian grace constitutes us as friends of God, and its deepest tendency is to mystical love even unto the folly of the cross. No more is it enough to have a profound readiness (never to be actualized) for sacrifice and (radically and only hypothetically) for courageous endurance in love even of all manner of suffering and physical death. Now this Christian love always entails an actual sacrifice, so that every man old enough to understand must face the prospect of suffering, constant struggle, and death and adopt his own freely chosen attitude towards sacrifice, an attitude that is ultimately born of grace or of the rejection of grace.

It does not matter that these laws of human existence and of

37

the grace of Christ are only vaguely, if at all, articulated for so many of the billions of persons in the world who are not touched by the teaching and preaching of the Gospel. They are neverthe-less operative for all men everywhere, even though their reality be only obscurely perceived in the depth of the heart and soul. Our being in the world is signed with the cross. Who does not encounter every day little frustrations? Our very deepest tend-ency and drive towards unity and final happiness finds itself ever checked by the physical necessities of our lives as well as by the continuing moral struggle that every serious-minded person must always face. These profound truths of the cross that signs all human existence are of course perceived in varying depth and clarity, but perhaps nowhere as deeply as among the Hindus and Buddhists, who have even come to regard multiplicity itself as the root of human suffering.

Further, the grace of Christ that will deliver us through the cross itself to salvation in God reveals to us an even more radi-cally and essentially crucifying aspect of our existence. The dominion of this grace in man can come about only through crucifixion (at least, once man grows beyond infancy). If our human nature were simply open to and under the supernatural grace of Adam, this is no longer true as regards the grace of Christ. This grace of Christ is given to us, takes us, as we are, without any miraculous reintegration of all the various drives and tendencies of man into harmonious subordination to super-natural charity. This reintegration remains as one of our own great tasks to be achieved in the course of our lives, with the help of the grace that is always offered to us. But the resistance of fallen nature is only too apparent, and can only be overcome through long struggle. (If there should be in some cases some kind of moral miracle that makes a saint in an instant or in a very short time, this too will soon be seen to call for other kinds of crucifixion and sacrificial love.) Deep inclinations ordinarily remain in man to center everything in the world around the self, to be a law unto oneself in one's life. These inclinations remain to testify to our fallenness and to the resultant disorder that it has introduced into our being.

In this light, the grace of Christ is ontologically constituted with a crucifying character. This crucifying character arises in virtue of the necessary relation of resistance and non-integration of our human mode of fallen being in regard to the life of grace, and also in virtue of the constitution of this human nature in a state of suffering and tendency towards death that remains even under the dominion of grace. If this prior constitution of human nature in a state of suffering and tendency towards death does not in fact depend upon grace itself, nevertheless the grace of Christ that is offered to man must of necessity be a grace *for* living in and accepting in love such a human condition, and therefore a crucifying grace leading to love that embraces the folly of the cross in sacrifice and immolation. Both the first, intrinsic reason in the very structure of nature in relation to grace in fallen man and the second, extrinsic reason in the conditions of this fallen nature itself, mean that the law of Christian grace that leads all men to salvation in communion with God is also a law of crucifixion. But if it is a law of crucifixion, it is by that very fact a law that draws men towards a greater height and intensity of love of God than would have existed otherwise even in the original state of the grace of Adam.

If the grace of Christ thus responds to the existential condition of man, and to the necessary relations of fallen nature to supernatural grace in any redeemed state that is fundamentally continuous with the prior fallen state, then the idea of redemption through suffering and through a suffering Messiah becomes understandable as a most appropriate plan to remedy human fallenness. The redeemer becomes man in a way thoroughly in keeping with the existential condition of man—and indeed of man precisely as invited and drawn by supernatural grace. But this condition is of necessity a condition of suffering and even of death; and if Christ actually achieves the redemption of man precisely through the very suffering and death to which all men are subject, then he is most truly a man who redeems men in a manner befitting man. Through such a redemption of man he becomes at once the cause and the exemplar of that supernatural life to which all men are called. In his suffering and death he has taken on the conditions not just of fallen man but even of redeemed man on his way to God in virtue of the grace of Christ.

If we were to speak in an abstract way, we could say that Christ did not *have* to suffer and to die. Clearly, he could have redeemed us in some other manner. Indeed, he could have even achieved some kind of redemption that would have introduced a radical discontinuity between the existential condition of fallen man and that of redeemed man. But the divine will was to show forth an even greater power and an even greater mercy, as we have already seen, and to raise man out of his very fallenness to a new height of loving communion with God through the grace of Christ. But if this kind of continuity between the two states, with its accompanying "law of crucifixion," is to be maintained, then it is most fitting that the cause and exemplar of Christian grace show forth in his own life this very pattern of redemption through suffering and death, sacrificial love, and self-immolation in the folly of the cross. Of course, it was impossible that the resistances of fallen nature should be felt by Christ himself in the face of the grace of God. But he could face interior and exterior struggle and pain of various kinds, in view of our sins, because of our sins. By this very means he could not only achieve the restoration of man to grace through redemption but also declare himself and manifest himself as thoroughly and completely *one of us*, and through this total identification with us he might lead us into a participated share of his own Trinitarian life.

The suffering and crucifixion of Christ testify to us that he embraces our own supernatural "law of crucifixion," as the first to submit to it and even as the cause of its operation in other men. If it should seem that the physical crucifixion of Christ is really an excess, by our human standards, in his acceptance of the law of our being, we must consider a few matters carefully. There is already an excess of suffering in our poor world of fallen men, an excess that would perhaps be unintelligible in a "purely natural" state of man. But Christ declares his own homogeneity with our human condition, and even in its excess of suffering, in his own suffering and death. By means of this very excess he reveals to us all the more clearly the excess of his own and the Father's love for us. But he also calls us in turn to a corresponding excess in our response of sacrificial love unto the folly of the cross; for he offers himself as exemplar: "Unless a man take up his cross . . ."

The suffering and death of Christ were not metaphysically necessary gestures that we in any way compelled God to make; God always retained his transcendent freedom in permitting the fall and in deciding upon the particular redemptive plan that came to fruition in Christ. Yet we can say that the cross of Christ

41

is in fact both the symbol and the exemplar of the grace of Christ and its "law of crucifixion" that respond perfectly to the metaphysical structures of man both in his fallenness itself and in the face of a redeeming grace that introduces no radical discontinuity in human being itself as regards the conditions of its existence in the world.

The cross of Christ is, however, symbol, exemplar, and sign in many ways; it has a profoundly rich and multi-faceted depth of meaning, that is only hinted at in the analysis that has just been made and that serves our immediate purposes at present. A more adequate account of its intelligibility would require attention to still other aspects of our life in God: that Christ crucified is of himself a sign raised among the nations, a most appropriate objective revelation of the very mystery of the grace of Christ that has worked in all men since the fall of Adam; that Christ crucified prefigures even the visible life of his Church in the world; that he is a sign both of the evil of sin and of the detestation of God for sin; and so on. For us, however, it is enough to focus attention upon the way in which Christ crucified, and also in the rest of his human life, is the real exemplar of the full human reality of our supernatural life and movement towards God. All our supernatural grace is a share in the grace of Christ, and is therefore *patterned* after this grace.

But if every Christian grace is patterned after Christ's own grace, and if this grace responds to our human condition in such a manner as to be a crucifying grace, then we must also enunciate a general law of Christian fulfillment: Nothing is really achieved, despite appearances, in the supernatural life of man except through the cross, through suffering of some kind great or small. There may be much noise, much tumult, much show—in which

42

the cross is nowhere evident; but there is nothing really happening here for the advancement of the kingdom of God. Genuine success in the work of God depends utterly on the cross; and great achievements here must call also for great sufferings, for apparent failure, and for humiliation. All the rest is illusion. There is, of course, vicarious suffering, of which Christ himself has given us the prime example—so that through the sufferings of one man, another man's work may be brought to fruition. But there is also for every one of us the necessity of taking up our own cross if we are to follow Christ even to the fulfillment of the designs of God for our salvation. All this comes to saying that the Christian desire for the cross is not just a refinement of higher perfection, but that this desire is a consequence of any degree of adequate understanding of the real dynamism of the life of grace.

In fact, this same dynamism of grace tends towards a much broader and thorough imitation of Christ, so that the love and embrace of the cross appear only as the peak of a following and imitation of Christ that actually occupies the whole of Christian life. This is a matter of the logic of love, but this logic of supernatural love can be considered in two distinct aspects. In virtue of our supernatural, grace-inspired love of Christ our redeemer, we must tend to become more and more like him—according to the tendency of friends and lovers to become alike. The tendency leads to our adopting as our own the same values as those of the beloved Christ, even in detail. Yet it would be an oversimplification for us to think that this tendency simply leads towards thorough identity between our own interior life and that of Christ. We retain our individuality and personality, and each of us has his own unique manner of living the supernatural life in imitation of Christ. This raises a serious problem concerning the actual scope of such imitation. We must beware of attempting some kind of imitation of Christ that would be false to our own being in the particular circumstances in which we find ourselves. Such would be the result of undue attention to and absorption in the external details of the life of Christ, as a model for our own detailed action. These details are important not in themselves so much as revelations of something of the interior attitudes and tendencies of Christ. Clearly, it is necessary to make a careful and critical examination of this ideal of imitation of Christ by ourselves.

A more metaphysical way of looking at the matter is also possible. Our own participation in divine life through our supernatural life of grace is a uniquely individual participation. Even though the same fundamental supernatural dynamism is found in every such participation, even though the same fundamental values are values in every such participation, nevertheless we remain both free and compelled to pursue our own unique ways to God. Even though Christ may be said to have possessed this supernatural life in a plenitude that in some manner not only causes but also virtually includes all the possible participations of it by other men, nevertheless this supernatural life of Christ himself is still after all a unique instance in a unique situation— simply other than every other unique participation by every other man. This means, again, that the imitation of Christ is no matter of following any ready-made blueprint. There can be no carbon-copy spirituality in the life of grace; the Holy Spirit seeks with our cooperation to make of each of us, according to his divine art, an absolutely original achievement in the kingdom of God.

Nevertheless, Christ remains our exemplar in the life of grace and in the whole of human life under grace. "You are to be perfect, even as your heavenly Father is perfect." "He who sees me sees the Father." Christ is a revelation of the invisible God, and shows in his entire human life the way in which we are to realize ever more completely that image of God which is our own being. Through the contingent details of his own life, such as we know them from the Gospels, he has revealed to us the concrete working out in his own unique circumstances of the dynamism of supernatural life inspired by the Spirit of God. Through our own contemplation of and reflection upon these details and the various aspects of this dynamism of supernatural life, we can indeed come to some understanding of the dynamism of this same life within us and some idea of how it should be expressed in our own response at every moment to the call of God through the concrete situation.

But all this is meaningful only to those who actually are living a life of supernatural love. For it is only the dynamism of this life that calls for and can respond adequately to the example of the life of Christ. However possible it might be for some men to admire Christ in a purely natural way, and even to seek to imitate various aspects of his attitudes and behavior in the world, such a natural perspective upon Christ does not permit any real understanding of the central mystery of his life that is summed up in the cross. Only faith can begin to understand this mystery, and only a faith that sees the cross precisely in relation to the resurrection of Christ and to the supernatural salvation of the world in Christ. Only supernatural love can pass beyond this understanding even to the actual embrace of the cross and the Christian life fully in the pattern of Christ.

Still, there are a lot of problems remaining concerning the actual demands that this imitation of Christ makes upon man and concerning the actual values to be pursued in our human supernatural life. Although these are no simple matters, and although it is only too easy for men to err by fitting the Christ they imitate into a mold that they have already made to suit their inclination, yet it seems possible to make at least a few observations about some more particular aspects of the imitation of Christ. These observations may succeed in clarifying some of the very areas that can be too easily overlooked in onesided emphases and perspectives in regard to the incarnate Word of God and the meaning of his life on earth.

Perhaps enough has been said here in general of Christ's redemptive sacrifice, and of the love of, and actual endurance of, sufferings, by which the Christian can enter into the redemptive work of Christ and himself grow in supernatural life. A more specific aspect of this side of Christ, and of the Christian, appears in Christ's predilection for the humble, the poor, the unostentatious, in his life and in his teaching. This predilection of Christ, and of the Trinity itself in its arrangement of the plan of salvation for men, is perhaps even more of a scandal for some men than his suffering and death on the cross. After all, at least the suffering and death on the cross did achieve a great work, the redemption of mankind. But what could be the point of an entire plan of life so opposed to our ordinary human predilection for temporal riches, fame, and power?

We might object to Christ that these things are not bad in themselves, that they are even perfections of a sort, that they enable us to have greater influence among men and even greater effectiveness in spreading the Gospel of salvation. Does Christ really intend that his own example of humility, of poverty, of

46

lack of show, of human weakness, of submission and acceptance, be followed by all men? He does recognize the necessity for authority in human society, and he does not seek to dispossess the wealthy and the powerful. But he demonstrates throughout his life his predilection, his inclination towards something else as better than all this—without which all human wealth and power and show is only sham and delusion. This something else is a basic attitude towards such things which values more than any of them the simple truth about man's own weakness and fragility of being, and which also values in this way those conditions in which this simple truth may be more clearly and profoundly understood in sincerity of heart. The show of wealth, power, and independence of itself tends to insulate one from or to obscure the vision of this simple truth about man and therefore to smooth the way towards pride. This does not mean that such human goods are simply evil or useless; but they are not the greatest goods, and they are more or less dangerous to the spiritual balance of the one who has them.

But the imitation of Christ therefore means making one's own this same predilection of his for the conditions in which we understand more easily the truth about ourselves and about our dependence upon God. This does not mean that one who has such things must necessarily renounce them, for they are part of the order of the human world in which we live. If the higher and better way in itself would be precisely such a way of renunciation, still it is enough for one to take those steps that will make it possible for him to retain his spiritual balance and sense of perspective, his awareness of his human frailty and of his dependence upon God. But surely such balance, perspective, and awareness must also mean an interior esteem and predilection

47

for the other way, even though one is not personally called to follow this way. Still, the choice of any particular individual remains a very complex matter; we shall say more about it later on.

The predilections of Christ, and the place of suffering in his life, must finally be set into the larger context of his fullness of perfection, both divine and human. He is God in human form; and if he never suffers any diminishing of his divine perfection, neither does he lack anything of the perfection of a human being. The very dynamism of supernatural grace itself tends towards the full flourishing and perfection of natural human life as well, for this human life is part of these very divine designs into which we enter still more fully in our life of grace. If there is Christian grace, there must also be Christian humanism, with complete respect for and cultivation of the values of human nature. Any reasonable imitation of Christ, true to his own divine and yet fully human being, must seek for the perfection of natural human life as well as for the perfection of supernatural life in man. But this means also a tension inherent in Christian life, a tension between the demands of nature and the demands of grace, between the cultivation of nature and the cultivation of the life of grace. This is already clear when we consider in most general terms the relationship of Christian love of the cross to Christian perfection of human nature. Two somewhat more specific aspects of the problem appear in the consideration of the relation between Christian mortification and Christian love of the world, and between Christian abnegation and humility, on the one side, and human personality on the other.

The Christian tension between perfection of nature and growth in supernatural life through suffering and the cross cannot be ultimately unresolvable. In fact, it was already resolved in the

48

life of Christ himself, but in his own unique way in his own unique situation. Each of us must achieve this resolution in our own unique life under the guidance of supernatural grace and and Christian prudence, but above all with confidence in God, who wills both the expansion of nature and the growth of grace in man, though differently in each of us.

With these most general aspects of the imitation of Christ in mind, we can make a few detailed comments concerning it—but always remembering that no amount of such analysis can ever tell anyone how *he,* unique and in his own unique situation, is to follow and to imitate Christ. Obviously, the very first warning to give in this matter is a warning against any attempt to imitate the external details of the life of Christ simply because they are the external details. This simple, unqualified, unthinking imitation is just not the point at all; it is at best a childish folly or a flight of fancy, when it does not become outright foolishness and more than an annoyance. Nor does the imitation of Christ according to enlightened faith lead anyone to a simple and undiscriminating desire to suffer more and more it-matters-not-what. This would be a pathological symptom rather than a mark of Christian perfection. But it is possible to have a Christian comfort in the *state* of suffering, even without further discrimination, simply because every cross can be borne in union with and lead to greater union with the suffering Christ. It is possible, and perhaps even ordinary, for the enlightened Christian who has advanced along the ways of love to desire even eagerly such a *state* in which the cross is always at hand.

Christian love of the cross must finally be characterized by abandonment to the divine will. For this reason there can be no unqualified adherence to particular sufferings, any more than to particular goods, for their own sake. Nor can there be an unqualified adherence to those objects of Christian predilection that were spoken of above: the humble, the poor, the unostentatious, the weak. Even these must be desired only according to the divine will. Even though such things are seen to be most useful in themselves for growth in the life of grace and for spiritual understanding, one might well come to understand that the designs of God lead him towards a life of earthly fame, wealth, power, and so forth—itself to be lived for the sake of the kingdom of God. Even though one might come to see how the former means are most efficacious in their own ways in order to reach other human beings in really deep communication and communion in the truth, nevertheless it is also possible that God wills to use other means as well in the Christian apostolate. This does not alter Christ's own predilections and their reasons, and it does not alter the corresponding predilections and reasons for all Christians; but it does mean that even here it is finally not our predilections, however supernatural, which are the ultimate norm, but the will of God alone.

Likewise, if we are to speak of a Christian love and desire for insults, humiliations, and contempt—out of a desire to imitate Christ who suffered in this manner—we must again understand that this desire is not an absolute desire, as if these things were simply good to have. Such a desire is itself intelligible only insofar as our grace-inspired loving acceptance of these sufferings does indeed make us more like Christ in our interior lives, insofar as they tend to lead us into a fuller understanding awareness of our actual human reality under God, and insofar as such sufferings may enable us to bear witness to our fellow men that we are indeed followers of Christ. But this last motive has its difficulties;

as a motive for *desiring* such sufferings it might better be left for men who are well advanced in the life of grace. Even the other motives are not luxuries to be indulged in by any novice in spiritual life. For real beginners it would be well to speak not so much of a real desire for insults, humiliations, and contempt as rather of a desire for the desire. But it must always be emphasized that such a desire and love of predilection is not precisely for these things in themselves but rather as *means* towards a state in which we can grow more easily and rapidly in loving communion with God and with Christ, and in which we can be of more help to others. It would only be foolishness and stupidity to look for such things as merely external phenomena that happen to coincide with some of the external phenomena of Christ's own life. Mere similarity of external phenomena is not what lovers seek in their desires to be alike, but rather a profound interior agreement of attitudes and inclinations. There is never, of course, any question of provoking and drawing down such evils upon oneself at any time, but only of a grateful and loving acceptance of them in virtue of a Christian predilection that is itself reasonable enough in the light of Christian wisdom.

There is, therefore, profound truth in the Christian ideals of imitation of Christ and love of the cross. But there is also found, not uncommonly, some tendency to real superficiality about the meaning of these ideals, a superficiality that leads to misinterpretation and to foolish and even harmful conduct. Too great a focus on external details leads to a foolish, if not phoney, attempt to put on an appearance without a corresponding reality. A focus upon the suffering and cross of Christ that excludes the larger context of his life and being can feed really masochistic impulses or stir them up, and can lead to a rather morbid personality. Unless one seeks to understand the deep roots of the behavior of Christ under the dynamism of the grace of God and the impulse of the Spirit of love, the actions of Christ, and some of his interior attitudes, might be imitated without any real sense of the underlying psychological unity from which they spring. But this kind of Christian behavior might well lead to the generation of serious psychological conflicts or at least considerable interior tension. It is the inner spirit of Christ, the spirit of charity in all its nuances, that must be sought through the imitation of Christ and the love of the cross. Without the continual growth of this spirit in us, without the help of the grace of the Spirit, we cannot really achieve any imitation of Christ that will be truly authentic. Without this spirit, we cannot end in anything but failure or self-complacency over some self-improvement.

Before attempting to apply in religious life what we have been saying for a better understanding of the ideal of imitation of Christ and love of the cross, it may be well to go back to consider some of the difficulties that were raised at the very beginning concerning both the imitation of Christ and the love of the cross. Out of these introductory questionings we can distinguish five principal objections:

(1) It is very difficult to arrive at clear and definite knowledge regarding Christ's own interior dispositions of spirit in the course of his life, beyond some rather general understanding. How then can we propose any realistic ideal of imitation of these interior dispositions of Christ?

(2) Since the life of every man is necessarily unique, indeed unique even at every moment in every situation, how could one speak of imitating Christ? Each of us must make his own unique responses to his own unique situations.

(3) Christ's mission to the world was essentially the spiritual one of announcing the good news of the coming of the kingdom of God. What can the imitation of Christ mean for those who enter whole-heartedly into the concerns of the world, seeking to fulfill a "secular" vocation in assuming their share of the common secular task of mankind?

(4) How can love of and desire for the cross be reconciled with the continual struggle of man against the evils of the world, and towards making this world a better and better place in which to live?

(5) Can it ever be intelligible for man, with his personal dignity, to submit freely to avoidable suffering, to real offenses, and to accept prospects of lower levels of human development than those which might otherwise be open to him?

Both the first and the second objections have already been answered earlier. It is simply not necessary for us to know exactly the moment-by-moment dispositions of Christ in the midst of events. What is necessary is to understand as profoundly as possible his most fundamental attitudes, which provide also for us light concerning the dynamism and values of the life of grace. These fundamental attitudes are what are important for us to understand, for it is in taking on these same attitudes that we can ourselves come to a fuller manifestation of Christian life in our own activity in the unique situations of our own lives.

The third objection is partially answered in the light of what we have just said. Christ offers to no one of us a ready-made model to answer every question of human conduct in every situation by providing a carbon-copy from his own life. But even if it be acknowledged that Christ's mission in the world was finally a spiritual one, nevertheless we must not overlook that portion of his life, by far the greater, in which he was occupied simply in living a thoroughly human existence at Nazareth—and with the "secular" trade of carpenter. It is not a new ascetical thought to call attention to the fact that it is this part of the life of Christ with which most of the human race has most in common.

The fourth objection rests on a misunderstanding of the meaning of love of the cross. The Christian desire of the cross has nothing to do with non-resistance or inattention to the evils that afflict mankind, nor does it mean that we should exercise no effort to improve the condition of ourselves and of our fellow men in the world. Love of the cross is really loving and grateful acceptance of a subjective state in the Christian and not a passive acquiescence in the objective evils of the world or a carelessness about the actual needs of men. Rather, our supernatural life of love should impel us in quite the opposite direction. If we continue to progress in our struggle to make the earth worthier of habitation by the sons of God, we shall no doubt abolish many of the evils that afflict us and that constitute crosses for men. But these crosses are really only "accidental," in the sense that they do not themselves arise in virtue of the very structure of human nature in the face of supernatural life. It is in this latter domain that the "essential" cross of Christian life is to be found, as we have seen.

The fifth objection cannot be answered by a simple yes or no. It is quite possible that in some instances a free acceptance of even avoidable sufferings, offenses, and losses is called for in view of greater supernatural good for ourselves or for others. But it is also possible, and this can only be decided by a prudential estimate, that an even greater good will result from resistance, or an even greater evil be avoided by such resistance. This course of resistance is in fact very, very frequently the more desirable and even the obligatory one. Indeed, this would seem to be the ordinary case, until there is rather clear evidence that more is to be gained by passive acquiescence, at least in the supernatural order of grace—as in bearing witness by one's endurance to the primacy of the supernatural, or to the reality of supernatural love. But these matters are very difficult indeed and call for lengthier treatment.

It is now necessary to turn to a more direct consideration of the place of the imitation of Christ and love of the cross in religious life. First we shall make a few general remarks about the relationship between these ideals and such religious life in general. Then a few more detailed suggestions will be offered concerning the concrete practice of religious life in the pursuit of these ideals.

Every Christian is in fact moved by the grace of Christ towards imitation of Christ and love and desire of his cross. But this is true especially of those people in various religious communities who might be called "professional imitators of Christ." It is true that the religious life can be considered under many distinct aspects, especially under the aspect of each of the three counsels and vows of poverty, chastity, and obedience. But in speaking of the imitation of Christ we are pointing to the most central meaning of the religious life, in relation to which all the rest must be considered. The significance of poverty, chastity, and obedience is that embracing them constitutes a person in a condition in which he can more easily and safely live a supernatural life in Christ, following the call of God wherever it may lead. But this can only be accomplished through the imitation of Christ and even the loving acceptance of his cross. We have already seen that this is possible in religious life, since the imitation of Christ is no matter of placing oneself in the very circumstances Christ himself faced in his life but rather of meeting our own unique situations in the spirit of Christ. Only a foolish romanticism would today look for some opportunity to live in the very circumstances of Christ's own life, as if everything depended on such a similarity of circumstances (or as if *anything* depended upon this similarity in any real sense).

What is needed to favor the imitation of Christ and love of his cross is a state of life in which one can never be completely comfortable in and adjusted to this world, and settled in it. Such a state of unease, attained in the life of the counsels, would be already in itself crucifying. But this does not mean that such a state of life is inhuman and contrary to or destructive of absolute natural values. Rather, the purpose of such a state is to orient those values towards assimilation into the higher life of grace, so that whatever one does, be it even eating or drinking, it is done for the glory of God. Even the value of human married love is not so much destroyed as "sublimated" into a far higher and more perfect loving communion with God. (Sexual intercourse in married love is not in itself an absolute value but one relative to this married love and to procreation.) Nor is the value of procreation destroyed, since that is a value for the race and not for this particular individual embracing the life of the counsels.

Nevertheless, the life of the evangelical counsels remains of itself an already crucifying love and imitation of Christ. This imitation, and the cross of Christ, are not further ideals but are already constitutive of the counsels themselves. The logic of love that impels one to the embrace of the counsels will lead much further along the way of imitation, and of the cross, all who continue to follow Christ.

Of course, to stop here would not be to tell the whole story, since we are also risen with Christ; but our sole intention here has been to show that it is quite necessary, if the religious is to be true to his commitment, that there be no illusions about the place of the cross at the very heart of religious life.

This has been a rather long and rather theoretical treatment of the ideals of imitation of Christ and love of the cross, but such an understanding of it as we have presented does have many practical consequences in Christian life, and particularly for our purposes here, in religious life. A few such practical consequences are offered here by way of suggestions for realistic pursuit of these ideals in religious life.

It is necessary first of all that those who come to be "professional imitators of Christ" understand love of the cross, and imitation of Christ in general, in full perspective. These are no matter of some uncritical and unreasonable plunge into the irrational by sheer force of will in virtue of the "dynamism of love." Rather, such attitudes and desires have very firm theological ground and very precise theological significance. If it is true in the metaphysical order that nothing can be really loved except insofar as it is known, this is certainly true here in the further sense that nothing *should* be aimed at without the light of understanding. In this matter of the imitation of Christ and love of the cross, the problem of retaining balance and perspective is very serious and very difficult. Who could count the multitude of possible aberrations that could be stimulated and produced by partial and inadequate attempts at these things? Even after as clear an understanding as possible is gained, it will be evident enough that the need remains for most delicate and precise discernment of spirits under the guidance of an experienced director, in order

57

to enable the individual to decide just how *he* must respond to his own unique circumstances. But clearly it is totally inadequate to tell beginners in religious and spiritual life that "Christ did these things; therefore, you too without further thought should be impelled by love to follow his example."

In such careful explanation of the meaning of the imitation of Christ and love of the cross, it is much more likely that a solid balance of spirit will be achieved against these perverse pseudo-victim-spiritualities and pseudo-mysticisms of suffering that are only masks for psychological morbidity and the whimperings of weak characters. And yet adequate understanding of these ideals does open the spirit to allow for the real possibility of special calls of God to some souls to suffer in a special way with the suffering Christ. Clear understanding will enable even such persons to avoid some psychological pitfalls that might otherwise endanger the purity of their sacrificial offering to God.

The danger of preoccupation with imitation of the external details of the life of Christ has already been pointed out. Such a preoccupation would be evidence more of superficiality and childishness rather than of any really profound spirituality. It is more tolerable in children than in adults.

Though one may read from time to time in ascetical literature about religious superiors deliberately manufacturing unnecessary and even cruel crosses to "test" their charges, especially if these show particular promise in their supernatural life, this kind of thing can be frequently reprehensible. If the one thus "tested" has much intelligence, he may easily see through such "tests" and be confronted with the choice of becoming a "pious fraud" by acting out the expected response, or of perhaps resisting real injury in one way or another and so losing some degree of his "reputation." It can be an essentially absurd situation, even if we do not dwell on the variety of sordid motives that may easily influence, almost unconsciously, the one who invents such "tests of virtue." The most ordinary way for us to help each other along the road of supernatural life is not to devise "testing procedures" of this kind but to show the greatest possible kindness towards each other and thus to enable others to see more easily something of Christ and his love in us. There are crosses enough for all of us, without any need for anyone to invent extra ones for those he wishes to "test," perhaps out of envy.

Nor should we be too eager to invent new crosses for ourselves (setting aside here the whole question of the place of mortification in Christian life, and the ordinary nature of such mortification). Christian love of the cross does not mean desire to be so weighed down by sufferings as to be incapable of any good thing. God will know what we can bear, and what we need; and we may be sure that in due time he will send this to us. Ordinarily, we need not be concerned to look for this or that cross; it is enough simply to be prepared to accept whatever God sends, and to find a Christian joy even in the midst of such suffering that is accepted as a gift of God.

There is frequently ample enough opportunity to embrace the cross in the demands of our work, to find it clearly bound up with our attempt to respond to our own particular call from God. This does not mean that the cross for us will consist in a more passive acquiescence in every manner of obstacle and evil that we encounter, as in misunderstanding and resistance from others, humiliation, even persecution. Often enough, the cross is to be found not in such acquiescence but in the struggle that we must make against these things in our work. There is the cross of simple acceptance and passivity in suffering, but there is also the cross of fighting against all manner of opposition for what we know to be right and for what we know we must fight. Frequently enough, the by far easier (and selfish) course might be simply to yield to opposition with a feeling of martyrdom and a sense of heroism, even though the real martyrdom and the real heroism would be found in fighting on according to our light.

But Christian love of the cross does not mean a universal preference for the more difficult course. If the cross is a necessary part of Christian life, it is not the whole of it. In fact, to take "always the harder" as a universal norm of action is simply nonsensical—as any attempt to put it into practice will easily show. Our fundamental norm is the will of God; and in the divine plan for human life there are both easy and hard things, both joys and sorrows, both successes and failures. Love of the cross does mean willing acceptance of the more difficult course, when this is called for; but Christian prudence and the light of the Spirit will help us to see just when it is called for and when it is not.

If saints have spoken often of how much they deserve the sufferings that have come their way, this does not mean that they simply "gave up" in the face of obstacles. Quite the opposite! Accepting suffering as the due of sinful man, they nevertheless did the work of God as they understood it, without regard for the pain and the cost. We must be very cautious in reading the rhetoric of saints and ascetical writers. Always it must be seen in the total perspective of the many diverse values of Christian life. If a saint exclaims that all he wishes and looks for are crosses and more crosses, we must not presume that his state of mind is indistinguishable from that of a thoroughgoing masochist. And we must not elevate the actions of an instant that might be most authentic expressions of Christian life for a given saint at a given instant to universal norms of conduct, or even to norms that might be applicable to any other unique instant at all. If St. Paul could say, "Be imitators of me, as I am of Christ," we might profit from a comparison of Christ's mild reply to being struck in the face with Paul's words in somewhat similar circumstances. "If I have spoken evil, give testimony of the evil; but if not, why do you strike me?" "God will strike you, you whitewashed wall!" It is not necessary for us to enter into any lengthy discussion of the reasons for each response. What is necessary is to understand that neither one, nor both together, provide us with a universal norm or pattern. What is necessary is that each of us come to understand the fundamental dynamism of Christian life and the whole context of Christian values. Then we can grow in sensitivity to the movements of the Spirit and the call of grace. "Do not consider anxiously what you are to say or how you are to say it; words will be given you when the time comes; it is not you who speak, it is the Spirit of your Father that speaks in you."

III.

FREEDOM THROUGH AUTHORITY

THE emergence of a new and fuller consciousness in the Western world of the dignity, autonomy, and rights of the human person has been amply described in a number of places. Especially in the post-war period has this consciousness seeped down to every level of society, and indeed not only in the West but in the rest of the world as well. Perhaps the very experience of the rise of the totalitarian states and the long struggle against them were a kind of object-lesson for all to see of the real value of the person and of human freedom. Certainly, the deliberations and decisions of Vatican II have confirmed among Christians these insights that are by now themselves part of the common possession of mankind.

This new consciousness has led to some profound changes in the manner in which more reflective members of human society view their position in relation to the authority that must be found in every society. For some, perhaps, it is a matter of finding a new hierarchy of values, of seeing that authority after all is the derivative concept, that the freedom and expansiveness of the human person are prior and that authority exists precisely for the sake of this freedom and expansiveness. For others, who already understood, at least obscurely, that law and authority exist as moderators of the prior expansiveness of being (and even the eternal law presupposes the divine being), there is need not so much of a new hierarchy of values as of a new constellation of values.

While a hierarchy of values simply rates the values in order of importance, a constellation of values does this but also much more. Such a constellation of values is a grouping of values that tend to be so associated in terms of complementarity, tension, reinforcement, and so forth that the consideration of one or some of these values tends to evoke consideration also of the others as somehow correlative, conjoined, or in some manner opposed. Such a constellation of values arises in a given cultural context, from many factors. A constellation is partially determined by "the nature of the case"; clearly, authority is associated with the common good. But other determinants might be: past history, more remote or more immediate; the prevailing philosophical trends of the day; the needs of the moment, as in a situation of war, economic stress, peace, or prosperity; needs-in-view upon the horizon; and so on. In the light of such factors, a notion and value such as free trade or respect for the rule of law or the unrestricted job-mobility of the person might be seen in widely varying lights, in widely varying value-contexts at different times. These varying value-contexts would not be simply a matter of differing orders or hierarchies of preference, but of various value-factors that would have to be considered, that would spontaneously or upon reflection rise into consideration together as intimately related.

There was a time even in American, and still more in European, society when such values as authority, order, the common good, and obedience tended to form such a constellation by themselves. It was not that the freedom and expansiveness of the human person were simply unrecognized; indeed, these may in fact have had fuller play in a less highly organized society than that of today. But when there was question of the rule of law, the above-mentioned constellation of values would appear without any prominent consideration being given to this freedom and expansiveness. The theoretical recognition, since the American and French revolutions, of the dignity and rights of man was not at all incompatible with such a practical constellation of values. This latter was very likely a useful balancing factor in the preservation of social order in such a free society. We are in fact disturbed at the recently manifested tendencies towards civil disobedience and the various forms of protest demonstrations of the past few years.

In the medieval and immediate post-medieval periods, however, such values as authority, order, the common good, and obedience formed the same constellation and without anything like the same recognition of the unique dignity, freedom, and expansiveness of the human person. In the religious context of the times, this same constellation included virtues like submission, humility, resignation. There was, of course, something of the perennial tension between the individual and society; but this could easily be regarded more as a lamentable consequence of original sin, without much attention being paid to another set of values implicit in this tension. With this tension, there had to be also a *de facto* balance; but this balance was always to be tilted, in the practical intelligence, in the light of the value constellation we describe. For men of these times regarded the order of religious life and civilization as something divine, something in its way more divine than fallen man, simultaneously imposed on him by God and constituting a kind of throne on which God might sit to rule the affairs of men. What was asked of man was above all conformity and submission for the common good of all; and this common good of all was itself looked for not in an expansion of the terrestrial possibilities of the human person but rather in peaceful growth in union with God precisely through such humility, resignation, and submission. There were, of course, those who would simply disregard this whole constellation of values and seize goods and power for themselves, in an assertion of proud independence. But they would also await the judgment of God.

It is not necessary here to pass any kind of value judgment upon such a conception of human life in society. It seems quite true to say that for men of those times such a view would not do violence to their aspirations so much as provide some hope for their fulfillment. If the cultural context and the constellations of values have changed, this would not necessarily mean that middle twentieth-century man is more right. Indeed, a mere reversal of the constellation of values that has occupied our attention: authority, order, the common good, obedience, submission, humility, resignation—to the anti-constellation: freedom, spontaneity, personal fulfillment, independence, authenticity, dignity, initiative—might not necessarily be for the better. If such a simple reversal has been characteristic of many modern men and nations, the results in exploitation, war, and the threat of complete annihilation do not seem to be altogether favorable.

And yet, if there is no question of complete reversal but rather of a complementarity—so that the same constellation of values now includes both the former set and the latter set, with a fundamental appreciation of the ultimate priority of freedom and the expansiveness of the human person—there does seem to be a definitive progress in our appreciation of "the nature of the case." We Christians have as one of our continuing tasks the synthesis of these value-constellations for ourselves and for the world.

There is more than adequate metaphysical ground for such a synthesis. The existentialist and personalist philosophy of the twentieth century has stimulated many Thomists to a fuller formulation of the metaphysics of the person. In such a metaphysics of the person both the dignity and freedom of the person and his relation to society, and therefore to authority, can be seen in such a light as to give rise to just such a broader value constellation as we are looking for.

The metaphysical analysis of the person cannot be presented in technical detail here, but it is possible to give a summary outline of it. We must begin by asking what there is about a person that marks him off as not only unique and autonomous but even endowed with a special dignity, a special call for respect. We note that persons are characterized by their unique conscious inwardness; they not only have an inside of being in addition to an outside, but they are conscious of this fact, conscious even of the very heart of this inside. This inmost heart of their inside of being is their subjectivity.

Now every independently existing being (existing independently of other creatures, though never of God) must have such subjectivity. No such being is a pure exteriority to others. Beyond the domain of communicable and objectifiable formal perfection in every being there is also the unique and incommunicable exercise of existence and activity; and there is also the unique and incommunicable root of such exercise that is subjectivity in the formal sense, that which constitutes the subject as subject. The inwardness of every being, then, is constituted by this subjectivity, ultimately by the exercise of the substantial existence of the being.

But this metaphysical inwardness is not of itself a self-conscious inwardness. For self-consciousness it is further necessary to exist in such a manner that there be no dispersal of parts outside of parts in extension. Self-consciousness, after all, requires perfect reflexivity in that which is self-conscious. How else could it have that complete self-presence of the whole to the whole that is the very being of self-consciousness?

Brute matter, and even living and sentient matter, consequently must lack genuine self-consciousness. It is true, of course, that sentient matter can have genuine knowledge of other things, and even a kind of self-knowledge. But this self-knowledge of sentient matter cannot be the perfect reflexivity and auto-transparency that are constitutive of true self-consciousness. The being of sentient matter is throughout a dispersed being, extended in diverse parts, even an infinite multiplicity of parts, that can never perfectly coincide with each other. The actual reality of genuine self-consciousness in man is one of the most certain indications that his being has something in it simply transcending all that is in brute and even sentient matter. This "something" is what we call the spirituality of the human soul.

We need not tarry here to follow out the implications of such self-consciousness for the spirituality of the soul; what are of interest to us are rather the implications of this self-consciousness for man's characteristic mode of operation and for his relationship to others of his kind and even to God.

As a consequence of self-consciousness, man can be said to be in possession of his own being; and this self-possession shows itself in the very real power of man to deliberate and even to say "no" to the various impulses towards activity that arise in virtue of the existential dynamism of human being as of all being. Such a moderation of the dynamism of being through the possibility of nihilation (a metaphysical "no" that is in no way a positive act at all) is the very reality of human freedom of choice. This freedom of choice is here seen to be grounded in the prior freedom of human spontaneity that is only the self-conscious self-possession of a subject-being endowed with a multi-directional dynamism towards activity.

The human person must dominate his multi-directional dynamism towards activity and greater fullness of being by freedom of choice. Through the responsible use of this freedom he must seek for and choose the course of action and the pattern of life that will enable him to develop and to expand to the full stature destined for him in the designs of God.

This full stature is primarily measurable as a degree of love for and communion with God, but it also has another dimension. Human self-consciousness is not only of one whose heart is made for God but also of one that is turned and opened outward to community with fellow men. Consequently, we see ourselves in a movement towards our final state with God not just as in a "flight of the alone to the Alone" but as part of the movement of an assimilation of a human community as a whole to God. If communion with God is our goal, it is also that state in which communion with our fellow men will finally be reached in its highest degree. But even apart from this final eschatological communion and community of men together in God, we are already at present conscious of an inescapable involvement with others that is truly a consequence of our human being itself. Our life of grace and love cannot be focused on God alone to the exclusion of our neighbor. That would be to live a lie. The Christian life of grace is an entry into the life of God and a sharing of his purposes and his love. But God's love is not for me alone but for all men and for all creation: that all persons and all things reach their fullness of being in accordance with the divine design that moves all men and everything else in its way towards and into the mysterious communion of consciousness that is our destiny. By our life of grace we are enabled to take as our own perspective on all things that of the divine generosity.

Clearly, the very first aspect of this generosity of love is recognition and respect for the uniqueness, personal dignity, and freedom of other persons. To refuse this recognition is to refuse to acknowledge the other as a person at all, to treat him as in some manner a thing that is wholly at one's service. This is a grave injustice to the other; but it also means a grave loss for oneself, a closing off of the possibility of truly interpersonal communion with another self like oneself, and therefore a closing off of opportunities for mutual enrichment in communion and communication.

But if the social nature of man calls for entry into such interpersonal relations and for mutual recognition of and respect for the uniqueness, dignity, and freedom of other persons, this same social nature of man calls also for a social order in which these same persons that are wholes unto themselves are also parts in relation to a larger whole. If each human person has his own immediate personal relation to God that cannot be touched by any other creature, still each of us is also called to God precisely as a member of the community of mankind and the people of God. There is need for a religious social order, and for the Church, in which and through which the immediate personal relation of each one of us to God is incarnated as of itself meaning more than just a solitary encounter of the alone with the Alone.

The freedom and expansiveness of the human person is thus at every level a freedom and expansiveness within a society. But such society always requires some form or order, and consequently some mode of authority to safeguard the common good of the society as such, which is a sum total of goods for the persons constituting the society taken together. Man's way to all the goods of human life is a social way. Had God not seen fit to establish a religious community with special divine guidance, surely man himself would inevitably form some kind of community to achieve to a greater degree the religious goods he seeks. Some kind of authoritative principle, and consequently some institutional aspect—at least minimal—is to be found everywhere in the religious life of man insofar as it becomes socially manifested.

Even in the pluralistic situation in which many religions are recognized as in some manner "equal before the law" and the right of private judgment made in some manner absolute, there is found something of this social ordering of religious life. Here civil freedom in matters religious is itself made an authoritative institution that regulates religious life in the nation as a whole, even though not within the particular religious groupings in the nation.

But the place of authority in social life must be seen to be ultimately that of a servant of freedom and of the expansiveness of the human person. The reason for authority rests on this prior being of the person; authority seeks to provide that order of life in which the free expansiveness of the person is allowed fullest play in the social context in which it must of its nature exist. This is not to say that the social life of man is secondary; the social dimension of man is given in the same self-consciousness in which the most intimate and private dimension of man is also given. But the order that must be imposed by authority on the free and social expansiveness and interpersonal encounter of men is secondary, derived from the demand for order that arises out of the being of any interacting multiplicity of free persons. The need for authority is thus a function of and arises out of the existence of freedom, not vice versa.

The internal law of our freedom itself, as a finite freedom that is everywhere conditioned by the whole nature of the one that is free, is thus prior to any exterior law imposed by external authority. And yet the internal law of freedom surely calls for the existence of such external law and external authority, insofar as this freedom is always freedom in a social context. The internal law also calls for respect for this external law and external authority, precisely insofar as they are really exigencies of the finite and conditioned mode of a freedom that only exercises itself in a social context. Only in the case of clear conflict, and only to the extent of such conflict, between the internal and external laws would obedience be withdrawn from the latter.

If it were objected that all this is well and good as regards merely human law and authority, but that the relations between human freedom and divine law are quite another matter, we must insist that ultimately this is not true. Though man is subject to the law of God, this subjection is first of all in virtue of his nature and of the internal law of freedom that follows from this

71

nature. No further precept of divine law, given in some exterior or interior fashion, could contradict this internal law of freedom, unless God were to contradict his own external law according to which all things are made.

Now the first law of the free being of the finite person is that of expansion and development in freedom, to the greatest extent possible. All further laws, that determine the direction and course of the expansion and development in the social context of human existence, are in some manner further explicitations of the fundamental law of growth and development. This is true as much in the order of supernatural life as it is of natural life. (But of course, those explicitations which are provided by God himself or by his human vicars might not always *appear* to be explicitations rather than obstacles to the law of growth and development. Yet we are in God's hands and must follow his light.)

The most fundamental values, then, *are* on the side of personal freedom, independence, fulfillment, spontaneity, authenticity, dignity, initiative. But if authority, obedience, and so on are derived values existing in function of the law of free growth and development, because of the social context of human existence, they are nevertheless true values that must always be respected by man and incarnated into his life.

Moreover, this whole consideration of the "nature of the case" as regards freedom and authority must also be supplemented by further consideration—perhaps dominant in the medieval mind (but nonetheless true for all that)—of the actual fact of the fall of man. Because man is fallen, because his intelligence is obscured and his will weak, exterior law and exterior authority do have a further value besides that of regulating the social context of human existence. In the actual state of man, the exterior law and authority also have an educative function both for the intellect and the will, through pointing out the right way more clearly and even through the threat of some kind of coercion or other. Even this educative function, however, is finally in the service of freedom and its internal law. For this function of external law and authority exists only in order that freedom and its internal law may be better understood and respected according to their true nature.

But when all this has been said, it remains that we must keep a balanced view, giving what is due both to freedom and all those values associated with it as most fundamental to the human person and to authority and those values intimately associated with authority and the recognition of authority. If the former set of values is firmly grounded on the deepest ontological constitution of the human person, the latter set is also grounded on the constitution of this person in a social context and on the actual fallen state in which this person finds himself. But clearly the balance here is hard to maintain, especially at a time in which we see a strong reaction, and even an overreaction, against a cultural perspective that gave quite insufficient recognition to what are finally the more fundamental values in the whole constellation of values centered on freedom and authority.

This cultural perspective was not unique to the Church—far from it!—but its effect was felt strongly in the Church, and in the formulation, over two millenniums, of the understanding of obedience to authority in the Church. It seems quite urgently necessary that some kind of reformulation of this understanding, on the basis of a fuller understanding, be undertaken. We would be quite happy if what follows helped a little towards such a more satisfactory reformulation. But our consideration is restricted chiefly to an analysis of the ideal of religious obedience, the obedience of those consecrated to God in the religious life, with only a few additional reflections at the end concerning the general question of obedience in the Church.

There are doubtless those who feel that religious obedience is not a viable ideal in the modern world. A metaphysical—at least implicitly metaphysical—view of the human person such as we have outlined might well lead them to conclude that each of us is so autonomous, his freedom of such value, his authenticity so important, that it is now really inconceivable that one man should so thoroughly subject his will to that of another as religious obedience demands. This would not be to deny the value of the obedience to law and to authority that is demanded in ordinary social life; such obedience is demanded by our condition as social beings, and also by our fallenness, as we have seen. But if the primary values in this order are those of personal freedom and the expansiveness of the human person, then it would not seem reasonable to make any unnecessary—in this view—sacrifice of personal freedom and responsibility, initiative, and perhaps even of authenticity.

Yet the primary values sought through religious obedience remain just as desirable in the light of the foregoing metaphysical analysis of the human person. Indeed, they appear even more meaningful in the light of such a deeper understanding of the dignity and freedom of the person. Few have ever sought to justify obedience in the light of a supposed worthlessness of the human person and his freedom. It has always been just the great value of freedom that has made the "sacrifice" of it through obedience the true holocaust that it has always been considered to be.

However great the value of freedom and of the expansiveness of the human person, it remains as true as ever today that in our fallen state we are apt to misuse our freedom and to disregard the fundamental laws that should direct human development toward the full stature of man under, and even in union with, God. However great a good it is for us in spontaneity and with free initiative to choose our way of action so as to serve God according to our lights, the Church still approves and recommends religious institutes, entered with spontaneity and free initiative, as excellent ways to live a life of service to God and man. Indeed, Vatican II only reaffirms the eminence of the life of the counsels, and especially in such religious institutes. This approval by the Church means that God can still be encountered and heard in the authority and regulations of religious life. Moreover, for the group-apostolates of religious communities, some kind of authoritative direction and consequent obedience remain just as necessary as before. The political, ascetical, and mystical reasons for religious obedience remain intact, if they do not become even stronger in the light of our fuller understanding of the personal dignity and freedom of man. This includes even a well-worked-out and balanced conception of "obedience of the understanding," provided that this is never employed to compromise intellectual integrity and lead thus to a more or less profound inauthenticity in action. There can therefore be no question of simply dropping the ideal of religious obedience as something more proper to another age and unsuited to modern man.

But it is a fact that the younger members of religious institutes

75

in our Western democratic society have a much greater conscious-ness of the value of freedom, the dignity and rights of the person, responsibility, initiative and spontaneity, authenticity, personal fulfillment. These values have never been *rightfully* disregarded in religious life; but it has been frequently possible for them to remain more or less in the background of consciousness of many members of religious institutes, and even to be almost eclipsed in some actual practice. Yet surely none of these values is removed by religious profession, by the vow of obedience. The purpose of obedience is that each person under it may be more surely and efficaciously directed towards a greater fulfillment and incarna-tion of such values as these; and the purpose of authority in the religious community is again that it should direct the persons of the community towards such a fuller growth and expansion of their personalities, in which alone they are able to show Christ to the world to the greatest degree, and through which alone they are able to become most efficacious in their apostolic, and even contemplative, activity.

Grace ordinarily does not work its best results in stunted personalities, in creeping or degraded personalities that do not realize their true worth. The great saints, the geniuses of sanctity and most intense lovers of God—people like Aquinas, Bernard, Teresa, Catherine of Siena, come immediately to mind—were also most *free,* most authentic, most responsible, most sponta-neous and creative, and so came to the highest fulfillment of their personalities in the line of supernatural, and perhaps even, frequently enough, natural good. It is this kind of person that must be the goal of both authority and obedience in religious life. Education for freedom of the spirit in God, and not just prepa-ration for smooth functioning (and all but embalmment) in some niche or mold, is the highest purpose of religious life. It is quite possible that IBM or General Motors could do a much better job of the latter, and perhaps without so much danger to the human personality—for they could never get so close to its roots as can the directors of religious life.

Happily, the present renewal in the Church is taking consciousness of this aspect of religious life, and many good results are already being seen. Thus many of the suggestions to follow regarding the exercise of authority and obedience in the religious life today are by no means new. What is offered here is not so much a number of novel concrete suggestions as a reasoned basis for them. Such a reasoned basis might serve to calm the fears of some that the ideal of religious obedience is being watered down or done away with, and also to encourage those who already "feel" the necessity for such a rethinking of religious obedience but have misgivings because of the absence of a fully reasoned basis for their "feeling." Such fears and misgivings are very much present today, even when authoritative sanction is given in one or other religious community for some such understanding of the ideal of obedience as is offered here. While it is no longer possible to be a prophet of renewal, it would still be most worthwhile to offer whatever might make renewal easier to carry through and with better results.

So there is not to be a retreat from the ideal of religious obedience, but a thorough rethinking of it in the light of the new circumstances of Western, democratic society. The principal circumstance here is that of the transit from the former limited and "slanted" constellation of values around authority and obedience to the broader and more balanced constellation of values around freedom and authority, such as we have described earlier. It is no longer possible for men of our time and culture to retain the narrower perspective. When we think of the exercise of authority and of the duty of obedience, we also think spontaneously of broader human values that all this is meant to serve. We think of the prior freedom and expansiveness of the person, of his responsibility and initiative, and of his duty to be authentic.

The mere fact of a command being given does not end such considerations; it is frequently only the occasion for them to arise, in order that the command itself may be better understood and evaluated. This does not mean that men with this attitude are more self-willed, proud, and stubborn. Rather, it means that they are perhaps more mature and more aware of the implications of what they do, both as regards themselves and as regards those whom they work to help. It really means that they are potentially far better subjects of obedience, since they will be able to enlighten the authority in many cases about aspects of the situation that he has not considered and since their final execution of a decision will be the result of much more thought and ordinarily of much fuller personal appropriation. Automatons might appear to some as more obedient; but in an age of cybernetics and robots one does not need such subjects.

What is even more important than being potentially better able to cooperate in the formulation of the command (in a material, though not in a formal manner—the command itself is always given formally by the authority) as well as in its execution, is this: the ability to profit more from the exercise of obedience in its ascetical and mystical aspects. The greater the consciousness of the value of freedom and of its related values, the greater the worth of the submission to God in faith that obedience involves. The more that one discerns such values, the more clearly he must also realize that he really does hear through the final decision of the competent authority the voice of our Lord. And the more he understands such things, the less likely he is to slip into the passive drifting that can so easily corrupt the practice of obedience, the more likely he is to understand and realize in his own life the real purpose of religious obedience—the fullest possible degree of the freedom of the sons of God who live in the Spirit. But surely all this is no dilution of the ideal of obedience; rather, it is an opportunity for a new degree of perfection in the exercise of obedience.

We can here consider briefly a few aspects of this new perfection that is possible in the exercise of obedience. First, let us consider the significance of the now clearer and more compelling consciousness of personal authenticity and integration as values that must be preserved in any exercise of obedience. Authenticity is simply being oneself in what one does, so that there is no shadow of play-acting or hypocrisy in one's life. (What is commonly referred to, for want of a real word, as "phoniness.") Integration is simply the extension of authenticity to the whole of one's life, so that every free activity does finally fit into a fundamental pattern that is fully consistent. Authenticity and integration are not just "good to have if you can manage it"; they are fundamental properties of the truth of the person, of what each of us ought to be as particular refractions of the personality of Christ, as individual persons each with his own call from God that must be heard and followed with his own response.

But to act without seeing the value of what we do is already to

79

fall into non-authenticity and hypocrisy. This does not mean that commands that are not at once meaningful to us are simply to be disregarded. But it does mean that this is a time for reflection, and perhaps even for discussion—to the extent that the nature of the command allows. (Obviously, we are not referring to sudden commands to immediate action that must of its very nature partake of the impulsive. However much we might prefer to avoid such situations, they are a part of every human life. But the necessarily impulsive reaction is the more sure according as the person who elicits it is more fully an authentic and integrated person.)

Where there is no sin perceptible, there is some kind of value in the commanded action. But there is still the problem of seeing this value for oneself and making it to be truly a value to one-self, and perhaps also of perfecting and increasing this value by careful consideration and by further proposals to the one who commands. This value must finally be personalized, so that the actual action will be truly an epiphany of the being of the agent and not just a sterile and automatic performance like that of a puppet. Such a personalization of value might or might not be easy in a given case, as in the general direction that one is to give to his life work.

But correlative with this need for personalization on the part of the obedient subject is the serious responsibility of the one in authority so to know his subjects that he can set them to tasks and give them direction that does really fit their personalities to the greatest extent possible. This is one of the principal aspects of the exercise of authority in a religious community. It must never be simply a matter of getting jobs done by it-matters-not-whom.

Obviously, here is a hierarchy of tasks; and therefore there are degrees of seriousness in this matter of personalization. Daily household tasks do not make the same demands in this regard on subject and superior as do major decisions that can affect the course of one's whole life. But neither subject nor superior can ever lose sight of this basic need for personalization as the presupposition of authenticity and integration; and both subject and superior must constantly strive for it, each in his own way.

On the most general plane, this need for authenticity and integration has always been implicit in the question of the suitability of candidates for the priesthood and/or some religious community. We have always understood that there are degrees of compatibility between individuals and such groups and ways of life. There is ordinarily a point at which a personality becomes, not bad, but rather unsuited for either the priesthood or some particular religious way of life, or even for any form of the religious way of life. We conclude that he would be unhappy there, and that he would have undue difficulty in himself leading an authentic Christian life there according to his own personality and the demands of living in such a state or group.

Something of the same consideration must be carried down to the more detailed aspects of religious life, so that the superior does not make it virtually impossible for a given member to personalize his obedience, or even unnecessarily difficult to do so. But of course, this in no way dispenses the subject of obedience from the continual, day-to-day effort at ever deeper personalization that leads to ever more complete authenticity and integration, first in the general directions that obedience gives to his life, and second even in the little matters that arise in day-to-day living.

But the ideal of personalization, authenticity, and integration

81

is not achieved in some kind of continual introspective concern to see for oneself in a reflective maner at every point how everything one does is truly an epiphany of one's being and not just a sterile and automatic performance like that of a puppet. Such a continual effort of introspection would also drive one mad or at least make one a little eccentric! What is finally required is that one really take on, as "second-nature"—which is to say "virtue"—a genuinely religious personality according to the nature of the institute. If this were simply impossible, one would really not belong in this institute.

Such a "second-nature" means that one's reactions in the ordinary course of day-to-day religious life will be truly authentic and personalized in a spontaneous manner; for now the pattern of such life fits the being of the one who lives it, by a kind of connaturality. The effort to fit into the pattern of life in this manner is precisely the required process of personalization of value. It is, in fact, called for in anyone who has ever entered a new social group. Of course, there are moments in which this kind of personalization is not enough, when one is asked to follow his own particular direction in life—but one which he himself has not chosen for himself and perhaps would not choose, or when one is called upon for some out-of-the-ordinary task. For such cases, there is always need of a special effort of personalization; and in such cases the superior must exercise great care not to ask for too much from the given person, and indeed to consider carefully the best means to insure the fullest possible personalization and consequently the maximum degree of authenticity and integration. For this is only to help this person to be himself in accordance with the designs of God, in his own unique likeness to Christ.

It may seem almost paradoxical to speak of preserving the values of initiative and independence in the context of obedience. There once was a time when a more passive attitude in the face of more detailed direction from authority was felt to be a good. Such a situation seemed to imply that there was more humility and more obedience than there would be with only general direction or a more active attitude. Perhaps this was very frequently the case for many religious; but it does not seem to be the ordinary ideal now.

For if the sacrifice in obedience is to be truly a reasonable one, then we must take into account and accept both the advantages and limitations of both subjects of obedience and superiors. In the ordinary case, both are adult, both are endowed with intelligence, freedom, and desire for the common good of the the community, of the Church, and of the world; and if each knows his worth, this is not pride but simple objectivity (which is humility). If it remains true that subjects do not have all the facts, it is also true that they may well have some of them and that the one in authority may not have them all himself. It is further true that such persons have minds of their own, with perhaps some very good ideas and plans of their own to promote. Such considerations make dialogue, communication, and discussion a practical necessity if obedience is to be really efficacious in promoting the greater good both in the work done and in the one who does it.

Moreover, the subject may be perfectly capable, and perhaps even more capable, of carrying out an assigned program of action himself, without need of any detailed program of directions drawn up by the one in authority. This is only an application of the general principle of subsidiarity. The superior should

83

not take upon himself the task of unnecessary direction, of giving really unnecessary (and perhaps also less competent) commands.

Obedience that has room for both initiative and subsidiarity is not a less perfect obedience but a more perfect one. It will call attention to the fact that a vow of obedience is in no way an abdication of responsibility to think about and evaluate even legitimate commands, and to reflect for oneself upon the real needs of the present situation and possible ways to meet them. It will make the personalization that has been spoken of above much easier to achieve in a fuller way. It also requires a good deal of humble abandonment to submit for formal approval by authority the ideas and plans that have been nourished and cherished in one's heart. The same is needed to retain real willingness to stand corrected for proposals and for action *after* we stuck our necks out by our exercise of initiative in making proposals or by our exercise of independence in the scope of action allowed us by the principle of subsidiarity, when such correction should prove necessary. And such an obedience will also make for better results in work, and for a continuing growth and development of the personality in the face of the various challenges that it must confront in the course of life. With such a notion of obedience, there would be far less temptation for some religious to avoid the necessity for personal decisions and personal responsibility, in a kind of passive waiting on the word of the superior—a waiting which could even take the especially perverse form of doing nothing especially worthwhile until one hears some kind of authoritative command.

Such an approach to obedience as we describe must also show the greatest regard for the primary role of the individual agent in

the individual situation. He continues to be personally responsible for the way in which he acts in this situation, notwithstanding the directive of authority. He continues to be called to
the greater good in such a situation. It is true that this would
not justify the subject in his simple departure from what has
been commanded, on the ground of some supposed—though not
verified—inspiration of the Holy Spirit. But it does mean that
one must be attentive to the movement of the Spirit and the
light of native intelligence not only in the superior but also in
the subject, and that final judgment and command should when
possible arise out of a consideration of the light that both have
to offer. One may say that the guidance of the Spirit here is not
to be found in its fullness except in both taken together (though
of course the formal prerogative of command is reserved to the
one in authority).

This means a considerably broader concept of the capacity and
duty of "representation" than that which we sometimes find. It
is not that the subject objects only when he apprehends a command to be clearly sinful, or that he makes his contribution
to fuller understanding of the situation only after the command
has been given. Rather, he must actually cooperate with the
superior in arriving at the final determination. It is true that the
superior ultimately has the formal role; he must finally determine
what is to be done. But this can only be done properly if the
genuine material role of the subject be respected.

While there are matters that obviously require no consultation,
there are also matters that can only be adequately considered
by taking into account the information, views, and needs of the
subject; and this is true not only in the case of individual persons
but also of the community as a whole. There are times when the

85

entire community ought to be consulted, either individually or as a group. Of course, the superior must care not only for the individual good but also for the common good; but it is not at all true that he alone is able to know and to care for this common good. But if this is an insistence on a real right of the subject to be heard, it is also a call to the responsibility of subjects and communities to reflect on such matters as arise and to make known to the superior, to the extent that seems useful and profitable, the results of their reflection. Obviously, there is here great need of discretion and balance in both superior and subject, not to speak of mutual respect and tact.

Closely related to respect for the primary place of the individual agent who must act in the individual situation is the need for authority to refrain from imposing obligations and making commands in some domains. This is true not only as regards purely internal matters of conscience, where such commands would have simply no force at all, and as regards external acts like the casting of a civil or ecclesiastical ballot, that of their very nature flow directly from an internal judgment of conscience and again would not be in any way subject to such a command, but also as regards wide areas of human activity that are too intimate and personal to be properly regulated by such means. For example, the precise time of some spiritual exercises perhaps ought to be much more a matter of individual discretion (though this does not preclude assigning a certain period as in general more favorable or more preferred, and consequently calling for more than the ordinary conditions of silence in the house). Or perhaps the hours of rising and retiring are just too much an individual concern to call for anything except some general advice rather than a precise note on a daily order. But be it noted that there is not question here of concessions so much as a situation in which too precise and detailed a regulation might become a simply unreasonable imposition, one that fails to take into account the unavoidable fact of human differences. It should not be necessary to go further here into the wide range of possibilities, from the unreasonable imposition to the merely silly custom that is nevertheless insisted upon.

Also related to this primary personal responsibility of the one who must act in the individual situation, even though he be commanded, is the matter of conscientious objection. In the ordinary case, the occasion for such a conflict between the conscience of a subject and the command of the superior should not be allowed to arise. If the regard of both subject and superior for the values of authenticity, integration, personalization, and responsibility is also enlightened by continual dialogue, it should be possible for the most part to avoid this conflict. So far as possible, the superior should simply refrain from giving a command that would create such a conflict for a given individual. Clearly, such an occasion could be circumvented in many instances by reassignment of the one in question, or by finding another man to do a particular job. But the concrete likelihood of conscientious objection in a given instance should also be an occasion for the superior to weigh seriously the reasons that one might have for such conscientious objection, which sometimes might even aid in enlightening his own conscience.

If the conflict cannot be avoided, and all appeals to higher authority by the subject are exhausted and fruitless, then there is need for the authority itself to call in others to consider the conflict and to suggest possible courses of action to both subject and superior. (The recent legislation of the XXXI General Congregation of the Society of Jesus makes provision for such action in the Society, even to the extent of calling in someone from outside the Society itself.) Perhaps this means will finally resolve the problem. If it does not, then it seems that the time has come for such a subject, with as much good will as possible on all sides, be freed from his vows so that he may follow the light of his conscience in a more untroubled manner.

The most important aspect of religious obedience in the light of our new constellation of values is its significance as a *means* and not an end. It is of its nature a means to the growth and development of the person and of true personal freedom of spirit in the love and service of God. It must lead to greater love, but it would not do this if it were to result in seriously stunting this personal growth and in creating neurotic dependency rather than a fuller freedom of the spirit in the service of God. Mere mechanical performance in a "rut" might sometimes look like humble, devoted service and ascetical success, but it could just as well result from numbness and even a certain indifference that can arise in slaves of a system. This would not be a life of love, or at least not a life of very vital and intense love.

Such comments as these do not throw the burden of the effort mainly on superiors, however. It is true that they must take care that they use their authority and the instrument of obedience to help religious grow more surely and more fully into men and women completely in love with God and devoted to his service, and to avoid so far as they can the perversion of this powerful ascetical, and even mystical, instrument; but the primary burden is still on the subject of obedience, who must continually strive to see the place and use of obedience in his life. It is not an escape from responsibility and from the necessity of personal growth and development to full freedom of spirit. It is, however, still a very great value, in the context of the whole value constellation of which we have spoken so much, that is still at present what it has been in the past, an efficacious means of personal growth in Christian life and Christian freedom of spirit.

If obedience was so powerful a means in the past, notwithstanding an inadequate explicitation of its larger context, it can be even more effective at present and in the future, in the light of the further explicitation of this context that has become possible in the twentieth century. From this perspective, religious obedience is much more than a "viable ideal" in the modern world. It can be now even more fully what it has always been— a way to the highest perfection of human personality even in the natural order but especially in the supernatural life of love and service of both God and man.

Is it possible for such a conception of religious obedience as we have been describing really to become widespread in the Church? In fact, we can already see it in many younger religious, who do not yet possess authority in their communities, and in more than a few of those who do have authority.

This does not mean that the older view was "wrong." Rather, it means that the development of human culture also permits further development and perfection of the forms and means of spiritual life. Surely, this should not be unexpected or unwelcome. Such a move towards a fuller freedom of the spirit under obedience is called for by the signs of the times. But it is also in deepest accordance with the fundamental dynamism of the life of grace, that grace the first effect and last goal of which is a fuller freedom of the spirit for an expansive personal growth in the life of knowing, loving, and serving God.

There is a very real problem of adjustment to this development. There are many older men, and many outside the strong influence of Western social thought, who simply do not yet appreciate the idea of man that is behind it, for whom the new and fuller constellation of values around authority and obedience has not yet taken shape. Such a cultural difference calls for, and will continue for some time to call for, a great deal of patience and tolerance on both sides and a considerable and prolonged effort towards mutual understanding. Those of us who feel that "the future is on our side" in this matter must not fail to recognize that the great saints of the Church were produced by God in that earlier cultural context; we have yet to see the saints that we hope God will produce in the new one. We must still only *hope* to become religious as good as so many that have gone before us, though in our own somewhat different way.

The consideration of religious obedience that we have just completed has implications far beyond religious life itself. Surely the constellation of values around authority and obedience that has been noted here should have some impact on the exercise of authority in any sphere of human activity. But it seems especially appropriate to add here a few reflections concerning the significance of a "new spirit" in the Church. Still, in doing so, we would not wish to be identified with some post-conciliar extremists who seem to think that freedom means license for indiscriminate criticism, or even for doing whatever one pleases in a total disregard of authority and law in the Church.

There had been, in the pre-conciliar Church, something of an emphasis on obedience as mere, almost passive, conformity to authoritative decrees. One did see at times a use of authority that treated Christians as spiritual children who must inevitably stay that way, instead of educating them for spiritual adulthood and recognizing that in fact there are some who already are rather mature Christians whose views call for respect even from those in authority. Communication and dialogue were at a minimum between the Christian people and the authority of Pope, bishops, and administrative hierarchies. Possible organs of public opinion in the Church were kept, for the most part, under rather tight control. Subsidiarity was regarded by many in authority not as an ideal, but rather like a somewhat necessary evil that should be overcome as much as possible. Spontaneous initiative tended to be distrusted rather than applauded by a fair number of those in authority. The assumption seemed to be made by many that Christians would not grow very much in personal Christian life, and should not grow in interior freedom of spirit and capacity for independent critical judgment even in affairs of the Church.

But such a mentality was becoming increasingly difficult to maintain quite some time before Vatican II. With the growing postwar consciousness of the values on which we have dwelt so much in this paper, a rising tension between the aspirations of men more conscious than ever before of their personal dignity, freedom, and call to interior freedom of spirit, and the *de facto* regime of political government in the Church that reflected the values of an earlier cultural order, could not be avoided. In the providence of God, John XXIII was the man who "opened the windows" in the Church.

Vatican II surely produced a general program of renewal that is directed away from the older regime towards a new one that should have more vividly before its eyes the context and purpose of authority and obedience that we have described—the free growth and development of human persons towards spiritual adulthood with its possibilities for mature love and full responsibility in the highest attainable degrees of freedom of spirit. Perhaps it is unnecessary to dwell again on the details of what Vatican II has done. The "spirit of Vatican II" is very much in evidence, both in many concrete results already achieved, and in an even more evident vocal aspiration for more to come. In such an agitated time there are of course also those spirits that have not understood, and some call for the return to the old regime while others call for the virtual abolition of genuine authority in the Church. It is very hard to say which group is more to be feared. Perhaps we should not fear either one very much, but rather be patient with them, pray for them, parry them, correct them when clearly necesary, but "never take nonsense *too* seriously." They will settle down and adjust to the new order of things, with both its authority and its freedom. Or they will simply leave the Church, preferring their light to the light of the Church. They cannot be denied their freedom to make such a choice.

IV.

TRUE AND FALSE POVERTY

A GREAT deal of Christian asceticism, such as the ideal of religious poverty, has been ascribed to the influence of Plato if not even of the Manichees. Especially has this been done when there is question of a poverty based on the concept that the body is really some kind of prison for the soul, and that the highest purpose of human life is to achieve as great as possible a freedom from involvement with the material world.

There is no question but that the ideas of Plato, and even those of the Manichees, did have a great influence in early Christian thought. But there were in fact also much broader cultural perspectives that helped to determine the early Christian attitude towards poverty and towards material goods, the attitude which indeed has persisted as the Christian ideal even to the present. The great religious and philosophical movements of the last few centuries before the birth of Christ—among the Jews, the Greeks, and the Indians—had all emphasized the fundamentally spiritual character of religious life and of the higher life of man in general. With this came of necessity a warning of the danger of immersion in the pursuit of unlimited wealth and power. The example given by Christ in his own life was not something radically new in this regard. Thoughtful men were already quite well-prepared to understand this aspect of his message.

In all this was contained a profound intuition regarding the nature of man as composed both of spirit and of matter. This composition has as an effect a double inclination in man, one towards unity, the other towards multiplicity. The former is towards some kind of ultimate unification of his being in a higher consciousness in union with the ultimate unity of reality. The latter is towards the multiplicity that is first discerned by the senses and which stirs the appetite of man with an unquenchable craving for more and more of this multiplicity of the goods of the world. In order that the higher, spiritual inclination in man should succeed in dominating over the lower tendency towards absorption in the world and its never-ending flow of finite and unstable goods, it is necessary to resist to a large extent the unlimited craving of this lower appetite.

To those who would question the need for this resistance, it must be pointed out that man's only real hope for some final state of peace and supreme fulfillment must lie along the path pointed out by his spiritual drive towards unity in himself and with the underlying unity of reality. The other path only leads to endlessly tantalizing vistas of things that can no more quench the thirst of the soul than can those that are already possessed. To escape such a predicament we must hack away at its roots; this is the way to freedom.

In the measure of freedom that such a course of denial can give, it is possible to understand more clearly and to love more fully the real truth of things, however mysterious this and our final destiny may still remain to us. In this way there is also gained a greater degree of genuine freedom and independence of spirit, so that we can more easily make the choices that the degree of light we have may call for. One might even be tempted to hope that a really thoroughgoing renunciation of every finite reality (poverty carried to the farthest possible extreme) would lead to some kind of final emancipation from multiplicity—and so to union with the one.

Such a hope still beckons to many millions of people today. But we of course spontaneously, with our Christian reflexes, caution that some kind of balance must after all be looked for in this regard. Such an extreme of "poverty" is as false in its own way as would be total immersion in the unstable, ever-flowing multiplicity, if we are indeed not just spirits unfortunately imprisoned for a time in bodies but really and truly incarnate beings to whom bodiliness is as essential as is spirituality.

But in the profound awakening of human spiritual and religious consciousness that took place in India, in Greece, and among the Jews in the several centuries preceding the birth of Christ, there was no adequate conception of such a more balanced view of our relation to the material world. The basic intuition of the simple transcendence of the spiritual domain over everything in the physical and material world led to a rather onesided religious impulse and drive towards this height of transcendence—though in various ways. Something of this lack of balance had its impact even on the spiritual ideals of many of the early Christians. But this impact had to be mitigated because of the actual fact of the incarnation and also that of the continuing apostolic mission of Christians in the world. As a result, hyper-ascetics like Tatian and Tertullian eventually found it necessary to depart from the Christian Church in order to pursue their exaggeration of spiritual idealism.

Yet what has come to be called the Platonism of early,

medieval, and even modern Christianity did in fact come to determine the cultural pattern of religious life for many centuries. But one must be fair. Such a religious attitude (which we are here calling "Platonism") towards the material world is in fact founded upon some very clear perceptions concerning the existential state of the human spirit in the world. The pursuit of the wealth and power of this world very easily and quickly blinds one to the invisible world of spiritual values and realities, and success in this pursuit tends to insulate man from the full realization of his actual fragility and inevitable movement towards death. It can therefore bring him to a pride in wealth and power that is simply a deception. In this state it is only too easy for a man to lose himself entirely in "vanity," in contentment with and continuing pursuit of what could never bring him final peace, and of what is even antithetical to his true destiny. It *is* necessary for the wise man to protect himself from such illusions as this, by a cultivation of the spirit of detachment and interior independence from the fascination of wealth and power. Some kind of ideal of poverty, of detachment of spirit (spiritual poverty) if not of actual deprivation of material things, is a necessary consequence of any spiritual wisdom that looks beyond the multiplicity of the world to some final state of unity and union as the true good of man.

Christian religion, and other spiritual religion as well, has distinguished in general between two ways in which to cultivate such a spirit of detachment. There is the ordinary way, the more common one, of "careful use," in which one recognizes both his need of material things and also the danger they present to his spiritual perspective, and therefore endeavors to gain them and to use them but always in accordance with the religious teaching and faith that he has accepted as true. This is always a difficult way, since it requires self-examination and sacrifice, and a constant struggle against the unlimited acquisitive tendency. So ingrained is this tendency in man that we can speak of the "human will to power" as a universal category.

But the second way of cultivating a spirit of detachment from such things is even more difficult at first. This is the "higher," less common way of renunciation of everything in the material world, so far as the right of personal possession and domination is concerned. Difficult as such a course is, however, there is also the testimony of a long line of ascetics in many religions that after a difficult struggle this finally becomes the easier and safer way of meeting the struggle with the "will to power."

From this point on we shall focus our attention upon this problem of poverty, as a spiritual detachment from the attractions of material things, of wealth, and of power. We are, however, concerned with this problem within the Catholic Church and even more specifically within religious communities in the Catholic Church. Much of what is to be said must of course be relevant even in much wider spheres of religious life within and outside of the Catholic Church, but we shall draw no morals for those thus concerned.

When we think about poverty as one of the evangelical counsels cultivated by the religious communities of the Church, we ordinarily conceive it in terms of the imitation of Christ. We speak of it as of a condition that is favorable to a fuller imitation of Christ than might have been otherwise possible for a given individual. But such a manner of speaking raises some difficulties too. We must ask what precisely was the poverty of Christ.

97

Certainly he did not take any vows in a religious community, nor are we aware that he asked his apostles and disciples to do so. The poverty of Christ was surely a matter of an interior spirit rather than of some formal external profession. When we ask how we are to follow Christ in this regard, so as to gain his interior disposition of spirit in the matter of poverty, we must be aware that this would not be achieved through some kind of slavish imitation of the externals of his life on earth. Such an imitation of externals might be simply out of touch with the reality of our contemporary world—but Christ himself was very much a man of his own contemporary world.

Such a question must be pondered in the light of what we know of our full human being in the world and what it requires. Christ became fully and completely man, and our following of him requires that we too become according to our present understanding of man fully and completely human. It cannot be enough to ask what was done historically by Christ—like being born in a stable, and going forty days without food in the desert —but one must ask what a man ought to do now. We begin with a seed of the same divine life that Christ possessed in fullness, and we seek to cultivate this life that it may grow in us. But we do this with a much fuller understanding, in many ways, of the being of man than was possessed in the Semitic world at the time of Christ. If we seek to let Christ become incarnate, in a secondary and derived manner, in ourselves again, this must be an incarnation appropriate to the twentieth rather than to the first century. Thus it will be necessary to consider the ideal of religious poverty, not in terms of some imitation of the mere externals of the life of Christ, but rather in terms of what is more compatible with his interior spirit and conducive to our sharing in this interior spirit of his in the light of our contemporary understanding of man and his place in the world, even the world of material things.

It is of course still possible, though perhaps a good deal more difficult today than in earlier times, for individual persons to pursue an ideal of poverty in its purest and most extreme form. This could never mean the simple refusal to have anything to do with any material things at all; such is our dependence upon material things that an absolute spurning of them would only be one form of suicide. Rather, it could be the total renunciation of any permanent possession of any kind, keeping absolutely nothing except what is being used at the moment. Such a poverty as this, lived either apart from other men in the wilderness or by begging one's needs from others, is still a conceivable ideal of Christian renunciation today in at least some areas, and a form of witness to the fundamental truth of Christian and human existence.

But while such a course of action might be possible for an individual, and perhaps even a vocation for him, it is clearly impossible to think in such terms as regards those larger groups of persons that have formed around and followed some powerful religious personalities to establish religious communities of men and women in the Church. If such groups are to possess any kind of stability at all they need determinate organization, houses, resources for feeding and providing for the other needs of the members, and so on. This means that at least the community itself, if not the individual in it, must have some kind of permanent possessions, or at least a relatively permanent right to use things. And even the individuals in such groups are unable to follow an ideal of religious poverty that might be possible for an individual living alone. The orderly living of such communities would necessarily demand some elementary division between goods for common use and goods for the private use of each individual. If there is to be total renunciation of the possession of and dominion over material things by the individuals of such groups, this could only take place with the added simultaneous duty and privilege of the use of necessary things under and as part of the orderly life of the group.

It is possible here to ask precisely how "total" this kind of renunciation is in fact. But it is necessary also to ask how "total" such a renunciation ought to be in fact. In the nature of the case there is a continuing tension. Such an ideal of poverty might appear as, and even degenerate to, a simple program for a smoothly functioning "welfare society." It could in the concrete even tend towards a servile society, in which the individuals— having no economic independence of any kind—are simply treated as slaves of a system, to be handled and moved about indifferently at the wish of the superior. Such a situation would be as inimical to the free and expansive growth of the person, to initiative, responsibility, and spontaneity, and to true Christian maturity and freedom of spirit, as would be any totalitarian state—indeed much more so, since all would be done in the name of holy obedience and holy poverty.

Still another aspect of the problem comes into view when we consider the apostolic purpose for the existence of so many religious communities. In a simpler mode of existence in a pre-technical society it might still be possible to carry out a great deal of apostolic work without the use of many financially costly means. But this is no longer the case. Therefore the religious community must become involved in expensive outlays and the need of raising large sums of money. This seems to endanger the corporate image of the religious community in respect to poverty, and it also presents some problems for the individual member who must assume responsibility for and use both money and materials, while still pursuing some kind of ideal of poverty. Still another point for concern is the simple necessity in a society such as ours for readily available "cash" for anyone who attempts to function effectively outside the religious house, no matter what may have been the case in other cultures.

It is easy to see that we are here entering an area of most delicate balancing of many values and considerations. How is the ideal of poverty to be anything more than a myth? How is it to function in a meaningful and really effective manner in the modern world? It is very difficult to answer such questions in the context of an earlier understanding of the situation of man in the world. In this earlier understanding, poverty pure and simple could still be regarded as the ideal. Anything else could be considered only as a concession to the *de facto* existential condition of man. In a social order which saw man more as a servant of authority and order, rather than as the one for whose sake all the authority and order of this world exists, it was not difficult to set in the background the primary value of the expansive growth of the free person, and therefore also the necessary economic base that this demands. But in our present culture this is no longer possible, and the problem of poverty must be faced in new terms and in a fuller manner.

Moreover, the existential need of man for material things is not merely a *de facto* one, but an essential aspect of his being as a spiritual person that is simultaneously spatio-temporal. This condition of man is understood today more fully than ever be-

101

fore. A more adequate human self-experience, including reflection upon the meaning and value of technological progress, and a fuller metaphysical reflection upon this self-experience, reveals man as an incarnate person, a person to whom bodiliness is as essential as is spirituality. Man's actual way to God must be a way that is pursued in the world, through the things of the world, in communion with the other incarnate persons in the world. Such reflection must open the way towards a quite different view of poverty from that which grew out of the notion of man as primarily a spirit seeking to escape the material world or at least to avoid contamination by any more than minimal involvement with the things of the world. In the following section, we shall attempt to outline such a fuller understanding of man in the world and to present in this new perspective the fundamental problems concerning the possibility and nature of an ideal of religious poverty.

The primary metaphysical facts concerning man's being have already been noted above. Composed of both spirit and matter, with diverse and even opposed tendencies resulting from this composition—towards full unity and integration of being in union with God, and towards a multiplicity of particular goods in the world that is simply without limit and without possibility of ever really satisfying the drives of man—we are faced with the problem of somehow overcoming this opposition and bringing peace in our interior being. But such a peace is finally impossible for us without the help of God that is divine grace.

The way of simple and complete renunciation of the goods of the world through one's embrace of voluntary poverty, whether as an individual or as one of a group, appears to offer some kind of solution to the problem; such a solution seems to be in the long run easier and safer than the way of continual struggle to maintain a precarious balance and subordination between our various drives. But this solution opens the way to serious problems of its own, as we have seen. Clearly, only a few persons in rather special circumstances could follow such a way as individuals; and we have noted some problems that immediately present themselves to those who would attempt such a way of life as a group like a religious community.

The difficulty with voluntary poverty is accentuated by a consideration of a further aspect of man's being-in-the-world. His being is radically spatio-temporal and must, by a natural necessity, extend into a zone around him in the world. Unless he is to be left as a mere plaything in the hands of the forces of nature, which would be to disregard his higher dignity as a conscious person who is indeed the reason for being for these natural forces, he must exercise a domain over the things of nature, organizing them to serve his needs and purposes. The very achievement of some small degreee of control over some small portion of the natural world opens up to man the possibility, opportunity, and desirability of still greater control for a still fuller achievement of his purposes and fulfillment of his needs.

Through cooperation with other men, we can extend our effective control of nature through technology to a degree undreamed of in earlier ages. But such technological control soon makes it possible for us to aim much further than at the mere satisfaction of our fundamental needs as material living beings, and opens out possibilities of a fuller cultural life—and the leisure for it—such as could only be the prerogative of very few in earlier ages of human history. Such advantages are of course ambivalent, since leisure can be abused by individuals and since technological power can be used to subdue and enslave the human person as well as to free him. But it remains true that the much firmer foundation in material reality that technological control can give to our human being presents of itself an opportunity for the fuller and freer expansion of our spiritual life and the pursuit of its higher values.

It would seem, then, that man without material possessions, without dominion over material things, is almost nothing but another lump of matter tossed about by the forces of nature, with the aspirations of his spiritual consciousness destined to frustration. In this light the ideal of poverty might seem to imply even a falsification of man's fundamental being-in-the-world.

Such an immersion of the human person in matter is fully recognized by the sacramental economy of the Christian religion, in which material signs bear witness to and indeed are effective of the influx of divine grace in the people of God. This is the fundamental meaning too of the visibility of the Church; she is visible because she is an incarnate community of incarnate persons. Thus there is visible organization, visible profession of faith, visible sacramental life and liturgical life. So too, even the religious profession of voluntary poverty and the other evangelical counsels is itself endowed with visibility of ceremony and acceptance by the Church. But in all this visibility, matter, brute matter, must play its role as instrument. Any ideal of complete escape from material reality in spiritual life would not only be equivalent to suicide, but would also be a refusal of the Church of Christ. A poverty that tended in this direction would be anti-Christian.

This foundation and immersion of the human person in material reality also has some very onerous consequences for men in general. Human work is required in order to bring matter and its forces actually into the service of man and directed to his purposes. This is the "law of work," to which humanity as a whole is subject—and which very few who live outside the world of fantasy can afford to ignore for long. This means also a sense of insecurity for most men, a radical insecurity that not even great wealth and power could completely remove. Along with this sense of insecurity goes the felt need for concern for the future, for planning with discretion and foresight so as to insure as well as possible the continual supply of the material goods and forces that are necessary for the sustenance of man in the world. Trust in providence means that such concern should not *dominate* human life, but they are still demanded of men by the nature of our being. So also there must be a hierarchy of human values severely conditioned by economic and material reality. First one must live before he can begin to pursue what is useful for bettering his situation and to occupy himself with what is merely enjoyable of itself and without any reference to further use or to the necessities of sustaining life. All this is part of the common human lot. To be aware of all this is only part of being a man. Simple exemption from such concerns seems less than human, more proper to children than to adults. And all this— even while it makes it more difficult for him to concern himself with the great matters of spiritual life with God—nevertheless impresses upon man the fragility of his being in the world, and that he does not have here a lasting city. It also opens up to view very tangible areas of human need and possibilities for mutual help, the first and most basic field of Christian concern

105

as well as of any other form of human concern of man for man. How could anyone disregard the needs of his neighbor and say that he loves God?

Any fully realistic ideal of poverty as an ascetical means, as having genuine mystical significance, and as helping towards the proper functioning of a religious community both interiorly and in its work in the Church and in the world, must take adequate account of these aspects of human being-in-the-world. Such an ideal of poverty could never be allowed to obscure, and must make due allowance for, the real need of man for material means, for an adequate material foundation for his spiritual life and action. Nor should the concrete methods of striving for an ideal of poverty tend to lead to some kind of loss of consciousness by members of a religious community of the ordinary human "law of work," of the sense of insecurity and of human fragility, of the ordinary necessity for concern, planning, discretion, and foresight as regards the future, and of the ordinary hierarchy of values that is imposed upon anyone with limited economic means of support. Such an insulation from this common human lot would inevitably mean a certain degree of human immaturity and some lack of understanding of the real conditions of human life, even perhaps an inauthentic existence in a world that is more fantasy than real—more or less concealed by a feeling that one is only trusting completely in divine providence to receive all that one needs. Providence yes, but a providence that works through human sweat and human concern!

This would be a travesty of the ideal of poverty. The purpose of religious poverty after all is to help the religious to see more clearly than ever the real truth of the human condition in relation to material things, in a manner unimpeded by a complete

106

absorption of spirit in their pursuit. But the truth here is not that we do not need these things; it is not that they fall from heaven to those who trust God; it is not that such persons do not need to work or to exercise human care and discretion in the use of such things; it is not that they can act as if they had an unlimited supply of material goods miraculously provided by God. The concrete practice of poverty in religious communities must never be allowed to foster such illusions. These are not the serious thoughts of adults who understand human life.

The ideal and practice of religious poverty, then, must respect several human and Christian values at once. It seeks for a detachment from material things, a detachment that will prevent the religious from being so fascinated by these things as to become blind to and insulated from the fundamental truth of our human condition in all its fragility and contingency. Through such detachment, and especially under the guidance of religious superiors, the religious can come to a well-ordered use of such things in the service of God and man, well aware of the real necessity to use such things in accordance with the basic human spatio-temporal mode of action, and in accordance with the utter dependence upon them that is a characteristic mark of our human being. But the attitude of such a religious subject (and also of the superior, of course), and the manner of use of these things, must be such as to subserve to the actual growth of the person to mature human freedom of spirit under grace.

It seems that there is need in this regard for a certain commensurate freedom in use, which will be discussed later, and for education, perhaps in very concrete ways, against the growth of such unrealistic attitudes as those we have already noted. Such education might have many aspects, such as experience of actual poverty by living with the poor and as the poor, a course of studies which does full justice to the material economic bases of human existence, a theological view of man in the full light of the incarnation, and so on. But mere denial of material comforts and other material means apart from such a context of education would hardly seem to be educative so much as an annoyance, or at most a test of endurance.

In summary, when we think of the ideal of religious poverty, we think of the values of detachment of spirit and orderly use; but we must also think of the value of a *full* understanding of fundamental human insecurity in the material world, and of the law of work and prudent concern, as regards both the supply and the use of material things.

Actually, the ideal of religious poverty in the light of such considerations becomes somewhat similar to that of obedience, and it is possible to draw some analogies. Obedience does not do away with freedom and responsibility, with mature concern for what is really the right and best course of action. Obedience ultimately serves towards, or so it should, the fuller growth of free persons towards human maturity, independent judgment, and freedom of spirit. So also should the practice of religious poverty. Modern men, perhaps explicitly and certainly vocally conscious of their dignity and freedom, of their real worth under God, do not seek to abdicate responsibility in religious life but to grow in interior freedom of spirit. Poverty is not to make them mere passive instruments of the one who holds the purse, nor irresponsible spendthrifts, but to help them to grow to full Christian maturity. With this maturity, their own judgment and inclination will in fact itself be, and deservedly so, a not inconsiderable factor in the decisions of the superior and in the discernment of spirits that is continually necessary in the life and actions of the individual religious and of the community of religious as a whole.

Thus there is need for a thoroughgoing revision of a lot of ascetical rhetoric in regard to poverty. Sometimes this rhetoric has so much stressed dependence upon the superior as to give an impression—fortunately not often verified in practice—that religious poverty is more of a means of enslavement of the person than a means towards personal growth. Many "abuses" of religious poverty by subjects result only from profound consciousness that unreasonable and silly restrictiveness by some superiors is simply a perversion of the purpose of religious poverty. At other times, the ascetical rhetoric stresses so much the providence of God that one feels invited to cultivate a sense of financial irresponsibility that is ordinarily more proper to children.

The fundamental aims of religious poverty remain valid ones, and the theory of religious poverty as a means in the pursuit of these aims remains basically sound. From an ascetical viewpoint, poverty can still remove, if those who profess it follow out the meaning of their profession, the possibility of absorption in the pursuit of wealth, power, and the other goods of the world. Thus of itself religious poverty does tend to help safeguard clarity of vision regarding our relation to material things and to God. In the profession of religious poverty God is affirmed and embraced not just above all material things but even in foregoing all these things as the object of pursuit for their own sake. In a manner, the affections of the one who thus professes religious poverty are turned irrevocably towards God. So also, through the subordination of all use of material things to the decisions of religious superiors, one assures to a much greater degree that his use of such things will in fact be more fully orderly. The very living of such a life of poverty is already an attitude of both prayer and penance, that cannot help but have its effect on the world in the economy of divine grace.

From a more "mystical" viewpoint, religious poverty is a preparation for the intense and undivided affection inspired by grace that will make of God one's All in love. By the dynamism of supernatural grace we all are tending towards thus making God our All, but this tendency may not come to fruition in the present life. It is possible, indeed it seems even to be more ordinary, that we can be friends of God (through grace and charity) but without making him to be the All that is loved even to the point of what is simply folly by human standards. Jacques Maritain has spoken of these two modes of divine love in his recent *Carnet de Notes* (Paris, 1965). No mere vow of poverty, along with obedience and charity, could of itself raise one to such a degree of divine love as this. But to give oneself to religious poverty is to prepare for this degree of divine love by removing many obstacles to it. This is likewise true of the other evangelical counsels as well. Too often we dwell upon their canonical and ascetical significance, without the consciousness of the fundamentally mystical expectancy that is part of their very nature. The life of religious poverty, along with the other counsels, is life in a state of radical openness to the highest degrees of "love unto folly" that one is capable of and that God will give. It would be most inadequate to speak of the "state of perfection" without advertance to what this perfection of *love* really implies.

If religious poverty remains its ascetical and mystical significance, it also continues to have a profound apostolic significance as well. The abandonment of any idea of self-enrichment means not only the removal of a distraction to one's work but also the presence of a striking motive of credibility for the message that we bring to the world, the message of a God who does not care for human wealth and power but for the hearts of men. Economic dependence and community also tend to foster tighter bonds of unity (incarnating the spiritual bonds of community) between the members of a religious community, and so to make them more effectively one in their work for a common goal. Such a community can supply material needs far more efficiently to the group than would be the case if each person looked out simply for himself. But this means that the community as a whole should be freer to pursue its apostolic tasks.

The ideal of religious poverty, then, remains a powerful means of personal growth in Christian life and of apostolic witness and work. Indeed, it seems more needed today than ever, when we are so fascinated by our control over nature and its forces that we begin to lose our fundamental sense of fragility and insecurity. More than ever we need prophets like Jeremiah, who will call to mind the radical conditions of our existence as creatures under God, who will bear witness in their lives that the hills are indeed liars and that we must finally come to face God.

But any concrete embodiment of this ideal of religious poverty must give due regard to three special requirements, in view of the deeper human self-understanding that is characteristic of our culture. First, and above all, it must be understood that such poverty must respect and serve to the cultivation of the personal dignity and expansive freedom of man. Regulation of use is not to be sought for the sake of regulation, but out of intelligent concern for orderly use that will actually serve for personal

111

growth to Christian maturity and for effective apostolic work. Perhaps there is really no place for the concern that is sometimes seen for ever-so-small sums of money and expenditures of a highly personal kind. Perhaps more emphasis should be put upon responsibility in using money than on the necessity, and sufficiency, of securing permissions in any and every matter. Such matters are frequently enough resolved in the concrete situation by an enlightened and prudent conscience, but there is still necessity for thought and teaching that will catch up somewhat with the demands of real life in today's world.

The second requirement called for by our deeper human self-understanding is that any concrete embodiment of religious poverty must pay due respect to the actual fact of the immersion of the human person in material reality. The emphasis that is still sometimes found on the simple elimination of as much concern with the material world as possible, as the ideal of poverty, must be completely replaced by the concept of controlled use of that upon which, after all, we utterly depend for our being and for any action that is directly and truly effective in the world of men and things.

The third requirement is that we must constantly struggle against a mentality from which all ordinary human concern and insecurity about material and economic matters is excluded. As we have already pointed out, it is all too possible for one "detached" from such considerations to slip into a radically inauthentic mode of being and idea of life, a dream-world in which everything that we need is always at hand for us, provided in some marvellous but inexplicable way by the providence of God, a world very much like that of children in a rich family. It would be only too easy for detachment from material things to give way to attachment to such a wonderland as this, which would prevent real human and Christian maturity and understanding of life as it really is.

It does not appear that there is any simple answer to the question of a concrete mode of embodying a realistic ideal of religious poverty, one that will achieve the purposes indicated earlier and at the same time satisfy the requirements just outlined. It seems quite likely that in fact this question is not to be resolved in the same manner in every religious community, because religious communities have many quite different roles in the Church and in the world. But now that we have presented some fundamental values that are at stake in regard to religious poverty, it is at least possible to consider in a somewhat critical way some more or less meaningful modes of such poverty, central concepts or at least peripheral aspects of possible ideas of religious poverty. Though the actual combination and balance of elements in any more concrete ideal of religious poverty would have to be varied according to the nature and work of the given religious community, it is possible to see here in a rather general way something of the strength and weakness of each particular element.

Clearly, such a professed religious poverty must be dominated by genuine poverty of spirit, interior detachment from material things, and their pursuit. This is actually required of anyone who understands that we are not made for anything in the material world but for union with God. We may say that this poverty of spirit is also at the heart of the evangelical counsel of poverty; but religious poverty is something more, offering a surer and safer way towards obtaining this poverty of spirit. Yet beyond doubt the religious is expected and obliged to pursue this interior poverty with even greater desire and pains than the ordinary Christian. The way in which he is to set about this is in general indicated by the rule and manner of life of the particular religious community in which he is.

Thus it is that religious poverty also has the juridical aspect that is canonical poverty, poverty as a juridical norm that exerts its force on those who take vows within a particular religious community. Since we are speaking of the poverty of stable groups or communities, such a juridical aspect of poverty is clearly necessary as the external form and incarnation of the order that helps assure the stability of the group. But this external aspect of poverty must be only the exterior sign and partial safeguard of an interior spirit; without the interior spirit this external aspect would be only hypocrisy. In such a juridical and external norm we find only a set of "minimum" requirements that do not themselves constitute the ascetical ideal of poverty, but are only safeguards around it, signs of it, and invitations to it.

But now it is necessary to point out in specific detail the actual structure of such an ideal of religious poverty itself. One possible aspect immediately suggests itself; but it is one which has already been rejected for good reasons—except perhaps for some individuals following their own way at the call of God, whether they happen to live within or outside of some religious community. This would be the ideal of the renunciation of every material thing, so far as possible, without qualification, the ideal of poverty as complete destitution. Here one would own nothing and use only what is immediately needed at present. The dangers in such a concept of poverty have already been pointed out—we cannot ignore the human condition and its utter dependence upon and immersion in the material world. Our well being, and our path to God itself, require a material base and the use of material things. If some individual person feels that he has good reason to pursue such a path, as one called by God, that is an affair finally between him and God (though his relation to the human community, and to his religious community too if he should be a member of one, must be taken into consideration in any effort actually to follow such a way). But such could not be the way of any stable human group. And there is constant need for persons of a certain "mystical" temperament continually to remind themselves that man is not a spirit trying to escape matter and the material world, but an incarnate person who must live in and by this material world and so make his way towards God. A mysticism that would ignore this primary fact of human existence is simply not true; it is a pseudo-mysticism that will lead to physical breakdown, or perhaps to spiritual breakdown first.

But a genuine aspect of religious poverty is that of the re-nunciation of every material thing as regards independent pos-session and use. This is the ideal of poverty of dependence. It has an obvious affinity to obedience, in that it means that one's possession and use of material things is completely dependent—understanding complete dependence in a human and reasonable way—upon the rules of the community and upon those in au-thority in the community.

We have already pointed out at considerable length dangers latent in this ideal of religious poverty, dangers which must be both taken into account and warded off through the further aspects of religious poverty that will soon come into view. In summary, these dangers are those that are inherent in any paternal society: such a society tends to induce comfortable inertia into its members, and a spirit of servility that is inimical to full personal growth; and it tends to develop a bureaucratic structure that makes the exercise of initiative in action very difficult. All this means that real growth to full mature freedom of spirit could at times tend to be impeded rather than helped in such a paternal regime, and that apostolic activity itself, and especially the exercise of apostolic initiative, could tend to be seriously hindered.

But if these are dangers, they are by no means a necessary result of a poverty of dependence or of a regime of obedience. Were that so, it would mean that the very concept of a religious community living under obedience and in a state of poverty of dependence would have to be abandoned as an impediment to Christian life. But the Church has approved many such religious communities and continues to do so. This is so because it is possible to circumvent these dangers, and indeed it has been done. But to do so one must recall to mind a number of other aspects of the ideal of religious poverty. If some religious, and perhaps even some communities, have to some extent succumbed to some of the dangers pointed out, this is possibly because of an inadequate explicitation of, or in any event an inadequate advertance to, some of these further aspects of religious poverty. But the very challenge that is presented to religious communities by our more acute modern awareness of and sensitivity to such problems is itself a reason for hope that religious poverty will be able to fulfill its real purposes more perfectly than ever in our modern world.

It is thus necessary to clarify some further aspects of the

poverty of dependence. In this respect we can immediately exclude one possible understanding of the poverty of dependence, that which might be summed up in the formula, "Ask for each thing you need each time you need it." To some people this might seem, superficially at least, to be the very ideal of poverty of dependence. But in fact this would be neither practical nor desirable. The tendencies towards multiplication of bureaucratic structures and towards a servility of spirit that would make a veritable fetish out of as much dependence as possible are only too obvious here, to say nothing of the danger of the development or favoring of really neurotic attitudes. But it is necessary not only to see the unsoundness of such an understanding of the poverty of dependence but even to resist tendencies in this direction by less discerning subjects and superiors. No one is obliged simply to acquiesce in this kind of thing, but of course resistance has many ways (especially that of dialogue) without turning into open rebellion. In practice such difficulties are usually overcome through the exercise of common sense, but there is still need to make a really adequate theoretical statement of the poverty of dependence that would destroy any possibility of belief in such a mythology of this poverty.

The alternative to such a false understanding of the poverty of dependence is a qualification of dependence through the making of reasonable presumptions. This is a poverty of complete dependence, but in a reasonable and human way. It is no violation, but a contribution to the smooth functioning, of such a mode of poverty to follow the dictates of common sense in making small personal expenditures, or in using money to do what one knows he is permitted or commanded to do, without any detailed directions, permissions, or accounts being given—unless

117

of course the sizeable sum involved made some kind of accounting necessary for other reasons. Here, money and material goods are regarded simply as means and instruments to be used for good purposes according to reason under the general regime of obedience, and not as in themselves untouchable except in accordance with the most specific and detailed instructions and permissions of the superior. There is neither time nor energy available to intelligent and busy men or women to play a little game of never making a move, however small, or however necessary, without recourse to or without hearing the command of the superior.

Such an understanding of the poverty of dependence already goes a good way towards overcoming the danger of excessive servility and of excessive bureaucracy in the paternal regime of religious communities. We shall discuss yet another powerful aid to overcoming any tendency towards servility later on, but first we can consider a number of further aspects of poverty in religious life that should, when they are understood and assimilated by the members of a religious community, effectively remove the other danger of lapsing into comfortable inertia in an environment in which material needs are all provided without need of much concern on the part of most of the members of the community.

The next aspect of the religious ideal of poverty, then, is the duty of economy of use. How could religious poverty secure the orderly use of material things if one living under its regime felt free to make quite unnecessary expenditures, wasteful use or careless use, or even to spend money on utter vanities or on mere dissipation? The practice of religious poverty requires that there be cultivated some sense of what is really needed and desirable, as opposed to what is advertised or what opportunities are offered for buying. This should extend not only to the means used in one's work but also to modes of recreation and other such matters. Poverty of spirit is not really compatible with the desire of acquiring what is not really needed, or of spending money in mere aimless dissipation. A "poor man" must look for the "good buy," to "get the most for his money." Religious poverty would be susceptible of ridicule if it did less than this. In this sphere there is great need for personal judgment by each individual, though there is also much room for concern by the superior who authorizes expenditures.

But religious poverty should go even beyond economy in use to some degree of voluntary deprivation. This voluntary deprivation certainly ought not to be such as to interfere with opportunities for greater good in apostolic work or such as might even endanger one's health and ultimately impede the life of the spirit. Clearly this is a matter in which personal judgment of what is desirable ought to be the predominant factor (though not without consultation with the superior or spiritual director). But we really do need some kind of such deprivation in our lives. It is a sign of our absorption with God, that we really do tend towards him as our All, that we would really be content with his love alone without all our material aids and advantages. It is thus an affirmation of our higher purpose, a reminder that we cannot slip into contentedness here below, a reminder of God and of the cross of Christ—in which we too must share if we are to aid in any way in the salvation of the world.

It is also a sign of our fundamental identity with the poor, and not with those rich and powerful of the world who have made their choice and would live here forever if they could. Yet we

119

must beware of slipping into a form of mythology here. Our poverty of spirit, aided by the religious state, is ordinarily not an actual poverty. It involves a willingness, perhaps even an eagerness, for such actual poverty if God should so will by the circumstances and work in which we are placed. But in itself it is not actual poverty anything like that of so many destitute persons in the world. Of itself this "poverty" of ours is perfectly legitimate and useful; but to propagate such a mythology that would tend to equate religious and the destitute poor of the world would frequently be hypocrisy.

Religious poverty also carries along with it the necessity for some manner or other of work. One of the primary purposes of such poverty is to free one from concern for his own material welfare so that he may work more unceasingly and devotedly for the kingdom of God. This is most obvious in the life of the so-called active or apostolic religious communities; but there is also a "work of God"—evident enough to the eye of enlightened faith—that is continually performed in contemplative communities as well. The vow of religious poverty is no exemption at all from the human condition and from the "law of work." Far from it! Rather, those for whom religious poverty has truly been a means of rising to new heights in the love of God cannot but desire to enter more fully than ever before into his salvific work in the world. While we must be careful not to conceive "work" in some narrow sense that would ignore very real contributions in the Christian economy (like those of the contemplatives), at the same time there is simply no room for the idea that a religious community should be a haven for "gentlemen of leisure," free to follow their tastes in a wonderland in which all their needs are taken care of.

120

But along with this necessity for work, in accordance with the ordinary human "law of work," as well as with the dynamism of divine grace towards work for the kingdom of God, still another aspect of religious poverty goes hand-in-hand. This work is not a work done for personal or collective financial gain. There is a continuing need for financial and other material resources by the religious community, of course. But this need is not prompted by any hope of enrichment and ultimate rise to the highest social stratum and standard of living. Rather, it arises from the desire to continue, and even to expand, in an ever more effective manner, this kind of dedicated work in the world. If an individual religious, or a community, were to lapse little by little into the other way of looking at material goods, this would again be hypocrisy and there would be need of radical reform. A religious community must remain in spirit and in fact a "non-profit organization."

Implicit in what has already been said is the further requirement that religious poverty must be radically and fully selfless, with complete renunciation of any purpose of personal comfort and material good apart from the consideration of the work of God and of the community that does it. This of course does not mean that one will not benefit greatly under the regime of religious poverty, and benefit even in a material way. But such benefit is desired precisely insofar as it serves for the greater glory of God, the common good of men, and the common good of the religious community itself as an instrument for the work of God. No multitude, however great, of laws, regulations, and exhortations could secure the realization of this aspect of religious poverty. It is essentially an interior attitude of the spirit, that each religious must constantly strive to achieve and to maintain.

121

It is only one part of that whole reversal of attitudes sought for in all Christian and Christian religious life, in which God and not self becomes the central and preoccupying concern.

A further element of the ideal of religious poverty is the duty of generosity towards those in need. Needless to say, this duty is demanded of every Christian, for those in need are Christ in need; but the professed religious, one pursuing the way of religious poverty, should more than others be sufficiently detached from what he happens to have so as to be free in giving it to those in need. The need may be widely varied, from most basic human needs like food and shelter to the simple need of time to listen or time to explain. But if we truly no longer possess anything of our own, then we should be more than willing to meet such needs to the extent that we can, either by the provision of material or financial resources or—when this is what is needed—by the giving of time. It is only too easy for religious to become insulated from real awareness of such human needs, so that they simply do not realize the present need. One can be so intent upon one's work as to miss those precious moments when God would call us away from it to meet present and very concrete needs of those around us. (Less easy to excuse is the case of one who is too intent upon his recreation.)

This duty of generosity to those in need is so broad that it embraces too many areas and raises too many problems for us to discuss here. Yet we can note that it does seem that religious communities must make broad provisions that allow for great individual flexibility in meeting human needs. Rigid structures of rule, complex bureaucracies, small allowance for exceptions to the ordinary way of doing things, all this tends to make the individual religious feel very helpless about meeting the concrete needs of those around him when and as they arise. It is really a matter of seeing very clearly and emphasizing very strongly that all structures, procedures, and observances are really nothing before the fundamental law of charity. But this attitude must be carefully inculcated, and not nullified by the stiffness of a superior in accepting or refusing to accept explanations of behavior that goes beyond the rules—behavior such as is frequently necessary when the unyielding patterns of religious life are face to face with the variety and unpredictableness of life in the world.

Another aspect of religious poverty is that of common life in the religious community, life in which all are substantially equal as regards their material standard of living, in which all share in general the same material advantages or disadvantages. It would be unthinkable for those professing detachment from material goods to tolerate a disparity of social "classes" within the community, so that there would be relatively "rich" religious or "poor" religious. There are of course differences of needs, by reason of the work each one does or by reason of one's health or other considerations of this kind. These will call for some difference in what is permitted to each, but such consideration does not damage the integrity of common life. This problem of common life should never become a problem for those who have a real spirit of poverty; and yet sad experience shows that the danger here is one which must always be guarded against, both by individual religious and by superiors.

Another side of this common life is its requirement of constant concern for the others in the use of the goods that are common to all. Especially in the case of "common goods" in the stricter sense of goods that must be used by many persons at

123

various times—like the house itself and its furnishings, auto-mobiles, tools, the books of the library, and so on—there is continual need to regard the needs of others for these same things. This also calls for special care of such things, greater even than the care that is given to those things that are only for individual use. This is an elementary manner of practicing Christian charity towards our neighbor, and yet it is not so ele-mentary that it is not forgotten even by some members of re-ligious communities.

Further, any ideal of religious poverty in a religious com-munity must rest on a quite realistic understanding of our rela-tion to the world, of our material basis in it. There must be clear consciousness of the fundamental human condition that is truly universal and also sharply felt by most men: that our being is firmly rooted in matter, with consequent fragility and continuing need of material resources, but with limited resources to supply that need, and only at the cost of complex and continuing human effort. Unless means are taken to stimulate and to keep alive such consciousness, there is real danger, as we have noted above, that some living under the regime of religious poverty will actually fail to understand or to remember these facts of human life. Those who live in such an environment from the very time in which they leave the protectiveness of the family may indeed have an especially difficult time growing to such a realization. But it is possible, as we have suggested, to compensate for in-experience in various ways in this regard. Only it is necessary to aim at a truly concrete understanding of our situation, and not just at an abstract, theoretical knowledge that gives purely no-tional and not real assent.

Finally, an especially important aspect of poverty in an age that upholds the primary value of the human person over any system, even if it be one of religious government, is the cultivation of a sense of personal responsibility even in financial and other material affairs. Just as religious obedience does not remove but is in fact only another occasion for personal responsibility, so also the use of material goods and the expenditure of money calls for a sense of personal responsibility even in those who live under the regime of religious poverty. Each religious must come to see himself as an adult with limited resources, and must assume a responsibility for his use of such resources, asking himself much the same questions as would any other adult considering such use. The same economic hierarchy of values, between the necessary, the useful, and the merely enjoyable, must concern such a religious as it would concern any independent adult. It is simply not sufficient to make one's criterion for use and expenditure the mere obtainability of permission from the one in authority. The latter should be entitled to presume that such a sense of responsibility has already exercised an important check on deliberations and decisions to make requests for such permission. Clearly, there is need here for some kind of education to responsible personal use and expenditure. Various means to this end have been proposed—for example, having an allowance for personal expenditures, living independently on a fixed and reasonably small sum for a time, living with the poor and as the poor, and so on. We would not wish to make any concrete recommendation here in a matter that would be so much determined by the nature of particular religious communities. But still it seems necessary at least to point out the need for something of this kind.

All these aspects of religious poverty perhaps do not exhaust the possibilities. But when they are synthesized into a unified concept of this poverty, they can contribute to the avoidance of some grand oversimplifications of this religious ideal. They are in fact organically related to each other and not just a set of isolated ascetical practices or ideas; and they are by no means out-moded today, if the proper balance between them is maintained so that justice is done to all the values that are concerned: especially to our deep conviction that it is the person, his freedom, responsibility, and expansive growth to both human and Christian maturity of life and action that is the real purpose of all such structures and methods and ascetical ideals. All these things exist so that the person may grow to a greater fullness of mature freedom to give himelf more fully and completely to God in love, and so also to his fellow man under God. By such a standard as this, religious poverty like religious obedience remains a most efficacious means towards the fullness of love.

It might be worthwhile to consider the possibility of calling this kind of "poverty" by some other name. There are analogies, brought out in one or other of the aspects we have considered, between the poverty of the poor man in the world and the poverty called religious or evangelical. But in fact they are simply not the same. A regime in which material things are only means to use for present needs and for one's work, under the direction of some authority and within a religious community, is not at all the state of actual *lack* that is characteristic of "real" poverty. It might be that given religious communities actually share in this "real" poverty too, but this is not at all identical with the religious state of poverty. To avoid the appearance of hypocrisy or the danger of misunderstanding it seems well to consider whether it might not be desirable to avoid the danger of equivocation here and to use another name for the religious ideal. But we shall not even suggest one; that is left to the imagination of the reader.

Yet the analogy should not be allowed to disappear. Indeed, it will not disappear, if religious poverty actually contains the elements described above. But perhaps a consistent adherence to those elements would contribute to prevent, or to eliminate, some appearances of sumptuousness in communities and of childishness or irresponsibility in individual religious. In any event, the ideal of religious poverty is, after all, still an ideal. Poor humans that we are, we do not strive for ideals without lapses from them. What is really necessary is only that we keep trying, with continual vigilance and with continual renewal, and even with continual reform.

V.

CHASTITY AND
INTERPERSONAL COMMUNION

In recent decades there has been a gradual change in theological perspective regarding various aspects of human sexual love in married life—notably pleasure, procreation, mutual help, and personal love and communion. While all of these aspects have always been permanent in the sexual relationship of marriage, though not necessarily in all cases, it has only been in recent years that the first three of these have been given, theological emphasis. Procreation has traditionally been regarded as the "primary end" of marriage, but lately, in light of modern psychological and philosophical studies, personal love has come into greater theological prominence—so much so that some have wished to treat it as in fact the really primary end of marriage. In the light of the historical teaching of the Church this turnabout seems quite impossible, but it is at least recognized now that personal love and communion are not subordinate to the biologically procreative aspect of sexual life.

Interpersonal communion is one of the primary values of human life, and human sexual love is ordinarily the primary and fullest mode of this interpersonal communion. Sexual intercourse in marriage is the full incarnation of this sexual love in the manner connatural to the human person; it is at once a sign and expression of this love and communion, and also a means of intensifying it still more. When intercourse reaches its natural term in procreation, the child is a further expression and sign of the mutual love of the parents and at the same time a new bond that joins them still more firmly in this love, now not only mutual but for the child as well. Thus marriage and family life are most fully human, not at the biological level, but at the level of human love and interpersonal communion. The biological structure exists finally only in order to support such a life of persons in mutual knowledge, love, communion, and communication. From a purely biological point of view we might speak of the primary end of marriage and sexual intercourse as being that of the biological species rather than that of the individual, and consequently of its being found in procreation rather than in the pleasure and good of the biological individual. Still, this could hardly be said in such a simple way of the domain of personal and interpersonal values that are found here.

But if marriage is now understood primarily in its significance in the personal and interpersonal sphere (though without ever setting aside its biological aspects), this must mean that religious chastity also has an altered significance. Religious chastity still entails the denial of the pleasures of sex, the possibility of procreation, and the various joys of married life, but it must also mean that a primary natural mode of human interpersonal communion in love is excluded.

Metaphysical and theological reflection in this light reveals a most serious problem regarding the ideal of religious chastity.

We do not relate ourselves to God in the same direct manner in which we can relate to our fellow human beings. In fact, we come to know God through the analogical resemblance of his creatures to him; and we understand the meaning of interpersonal love and communion with God through our understanding of human love and communion. But if we are, through chastity, to exclude from our lives the primary mode of such human love, then how can we come to a most profound affective relationship to God? The purpose of religious chastity is to enable us, with the help of grace, to come to just such a deeper relationship of love, not only with God, but also with our fellow men. It would seem, then, that religious chastity really defeats its own purpose.

The problem is further complicated by the fact that the two sexes are mutually complementary in many ways, and really need each other in order to achieve full human growth to maturity. Without interpersonal communion a person must remain to some extent closed in upon himself, and, it would seem, thereby less capable of opening outward in the love of God. Still more, religious chastity tends, in the concrete, frequently to close off even other modes of mutual interpersonal affective relationship, in the interest of avoiding possible dangers of undue attachment to another person and even of eventual sexual difficulty. Chastity thus seems to weaken the ability of the person to enter into any affective relation at all, even to God.

There is in each of us a fundamental openness to God—even in the natural order and in the structure of our finite being, but also in the supernatural order through infused faith, hope, and charity—which exists prior to any human interpersonal relation at all. It is true that our supernatural life is thus intrinsically prior to and independent of any particular human relationships at all. Yet this supernatural life must make use of our natural knowledge, natural love, natural affective communion, in order to come to some analogical understanding of the meaning of the love of God, and to those particular acts of prayer and action that fill out our supernatural life under faith, hope, and charity. "If anyone does not love his neighbor, whom he sees, how can he love God, whom he does not see?" Full human life, and even full human life with God, seem to suppose profound affective relation to other persons, and perhaps even complete sexual communion with another in marriage.

Such considerations as the above have led some critics to suggest that the Church ought to reverse its centuries-old opinions regarding the value of religious chastity as a means of entering into a more intense life of loving communion with God. They point out that human persons are both spiritual and fleshly, that it is simply wrong to try to escape this fact about our being, that all men must work out with the help of God their salvation in and through the world and in and through their bodies as part of this world.

Yet the ideal of religious chastity persists; it remains one of the three evangelical counsels. It has had a long history in the Church, in pre-Christian times, and in non-Christian religions. Quite apart from the position taken by the Church in the subject, religious chastity could only be regarded with a degree of respect because of this long tradition in its favor in widely varying cultures and religions. It would be somewhat naïve for us to think that contemporary difficulties concerning the ideal of chastity are of themselves conclusive and that religious chastity has become an outmoded cultural and religious form.

Chastity has some resemblance to religious poverty. There is

in both a renunciation of the use and possession of some creatures in the interest of a greater freedom of spirit. This detachment from creatures is thought to facilitate attachment to God in
love. At the same time, chastity like poverty tends to enable the
one who embraces it to achieve a greater degree of order in his
love, now his love of persons and not just of material things,
and indeed also a greater degree of perfection in this love.
Chastity by no means intends to deny the need of grace-elevated
human love and communion. But through the renunciation of
sexual love, chastity prepares for a "mystical" love of God and of
all other persons in God. We mean by this phrase a certain excess
in intensity of love that is so focused on God that everything
else is loved only in relation to him.

The dangers of religious chastity for many persons have long
been known in at least a general way. The way of chastity is not
for everyone, nor even for most. "Let him take it who can." An
already neurotic personality might look to religious chastity as a
way out of some of his problems, but in fact will only complicate
them (though it is possible for some neurotics finally to grow
to mature persons in a religious life of poverty, chastity, and
obedience—but under enlightened direction). It would be possible for someone who embraces religious chastity to pervert its
intention by so turning in upon himself as to be completely
unable to relate affectively with other persons. Chastity can be
twisted into narcissism. Or it has happened that a person who
takes the vow of chastity mistakes the renunciation of sexual love
for a renunciation of any intense human love or friendship at
all. Such a person would be at least a stunted personality, somewhat hollow, perhaps almost mechanical in his life and work.
These serious dangers are further reasons, besides the strength

of the basic human sexual impulse, why chastity is not for anyone and everyone.

But with all this, the *theory* of religious chastity is fundamentally sound. It should lead, and has led, to a higher degree of detachment and freedom of spirit in regard to material things and the desires of the flesh. It should provide, and has provided, the opportunity for a new height of affective supernatural communion with God, and also with all men in God. It should offer, and has offered, a greater freedom for apostolic work for the kingdom of God.

The Church has already taught in an irreformable manner the great value of chastity as a means in the love and service of God; in itself the state of virginity or chastity is superior to that of matrimony for this reason. We have the example of Christ himself, of his mother, and of many of the canonized saints. In the face of objections concerning the "naturalness" of sexual union and of matrimony, we must first insist that the natural order is not all that is to be considered. In general, however, we must agree that successful human love-relationships (that are also desirable and licit) do tend to favor supernatural life with God and with our fellow men at the level of the reflex articulation of prayer and at that of particular action. They are even dispositions in favor of a good basic moral option of charity underlying all these particular thoughts and actions (merely negative dispositions if these relationships are not inspired by grace, even positive dispositions if they are in fact inspired by grace). But in order to understand fully the actual role of religious chastity in regard to supernatural love it is necessary to adopt a quite different point of view.

133

There is a love that is of its nature a unique love, without the possibility of any simultaneous analogues in the same person. Of itself it is a once-and-once-only affair (though it is possible for one such love to give way to another in the course of life, or in the entrance to eternity). Jacques Maritain has distinguished between an *amour d'amitié* and an *amour de folie,* to bring out this point. It is possible for us to take advantage of his elaboration of this distinction apropos of chastity in order the better to understand several aspects of chastity and its relation to our supernatural life of grace. Of course, not everything in our presentation is necessarily to be attributed to Maritain.

Amour d'amitié, or ordinary friendship, is less than *amour de folie,* though both would certainly have to be called friendship in a broad sense, since *amour de folie* is a yet more intense form of love that goes still farther, beyond ordinary friendship. But we shall set aside for the moment all consideration of *amour de folie,* and concentrate our attention upon various aspects of ordinary friendship, or *amour d'amitié,* such as is found to exist between human friends and also between a person with sanctifying grace and God himself.

When friendship comes to its perfection (speaking only relatively, since such a love could go on increasing without limit), there is profound affective communion between the friends. This communion also includes, both as a support and as a result, the mutual sharing of all their goods in communication and in other forms of mutual giving. What belongs to one belongs also to the other. And yet it could not be said that each has given his whole self to the other. It would be quite possible for each to have other friendships, at the same or even greater degrees of intensity of love and communion. Each shares all that he has, but not all of his very self.

Friendship between man and God means that the man has a personal affective regard for, communion with, and commitment to God that does in fact go beyond what he might have for any human friends. This is only to say that he loves God above all things, and would prefer to lose any creature rather than God and his friendship. Such a friendship with God already exists at the level of the basic moral option of charity; thus it might be found even in anonymous Christians who would not be able to articulate in their thought or express so well in their particular acts (at least not in such a full and conscious manner) their actual profound love of God. Such anonymous Christians do not have the fully articulated faith of Christians in the Church, but only an inarticulate faith-adherence to the saving good who is God. But those Christians who live in the light of articulated faith can cultivate relations with God even at the level of reflex articulation of thought and through the various particular acts that every concrete situation calls for. Such a fuller life with God, at the level and under the direction of reflex consciousness, would necessarily be understood and lived by analogy with one's experience of ordinary human interpersonal relations, further illumined by the light of faith. Clearly, every licit form of experience of human love and interpersonal communion could aid in enriching a man's life with God at this level.

But if there is analogy between friendship between men and that between man and God, there is also notable difference. It is true that such a friendship between man and God is simply compatible with profound supernatural human affection and friendship for other human beings. But at the same time supernatural friendship with God, in its roots in the basic moral option of charity, calls for ever greater entry by man into participation in the life of God. There must be a gradual growth of the di-

135

vine life in man, a gradual assertion of its dominion over every aspect of the human life in man. And although natural human tendencies continue to assert themselves throughout human life until death, these tendencies must themselves be elevated ever more completely by grace—integrated ever more completely into the supernatural life in man—so that God may have an ever more complete dominion in the human spirit in supernatural faith, hope, and charity. The fundamental tendency of super- naturally graced man is towards an immediate union and total communion with God which could not exist simply side-by-side with another such communion but rather must really come to dominate exclusively and in utmost intimacy—so that God really does become the form in some manner of the human soul. This kind of communion with God will be communion with God as one's All, simply one's *All.* This communion is already realized in an incipient manner through sanctifying grace and the in- dwelling of the Trinity in the human spirit; but it will be re- alized more fully, and more clearly, in the light of the immediate vision of God in eternity.

But if such a height of friendship with and total immersion into God in affective communion is not part of the ordinary course of human supernatural life until eternity, nevertheless the mystical writers testify that this tendency of the life of grace can be more fully actualized even at present. God does become more completely All for and in the spirit of man in the "mysti- cal life" and through "mystical love." (These terms are used here simply to designate a special mode of interpersonal relation to God, without carrying the weight of any special ontological ac- count of "infused contemplation" that would make a radical break between ordinary Christian spiritual life and the entire mystical life.)

This leads us to a consideration of *amour de folie,* or, we may say, "love unto folly." We shall examine the general character of this love, and then note the two modes in which it can come to realization here below. This analysis will help us to understand the precise role of chastity as a religious means towards fullness of life with God here below, and indeed also the role of the whole life of the counsels in this regard.

"Love unto folly" goes beyond ordinary friendship. In it there is not only a complete sharing of goods but even a complete, unreserved, mutual self-giving. Such an abandon in the giving of one's whole self to another is folly only to mere reason, for reason sees the *natural* reference of every human love somehow to the self (in the natural sphere, and without consideration of the fundamental tendency of supernatural life). To mere reason, love must always be the love of a good that is good-for, a good that is good in itself but also a good for the one who loves. But "love unto folly" goes beyond such categories of formulating and discursive reason, following a higher light of intuitive reason. And what is it that intuitive reason "sees"? It all depends on which of two directions this "love unto folly" takes. Before going into that matter, however, we will confine ourselves to some general remarks about this special kind of love.

In this love there is fully exclusive affective communion, not excluding other friendships but completely excluding any other love like this one. This is love of the other as one's All, and a person can have only one All, in whom he is totally absorbed and to whom he is totally given in all that he is and has. Such a love means complete communion of spirit and complete openness to communication and all mutual giving. Needless to say, there is no possibility of an analogical relation between two such loves in the same person simultaneously—there can be only one

137

All for a person at a time, unless this person be the infinite God who gives himself totally in all that he is to all men who will receive him.

Such a perfection of love as this could be found by man in either of two orders. There is a natural perfection (capable also of elevation by supernatural grace) of such love. This is to be found in the complete mutual giving of man and woman in sexual love in marriage. This sexual love is finally and fully incarnated, symbolized, and reaches its peak of intensity, in its physical aspect, in the act of sexual intercourse. But such sexual love is much more in the spiritual domain of affective communion. In sexual love of this kind, in which one person gives himself completely to the other in his whole being, there is the greatest other-centeredness that can be found in natural human love for another human being. It is to the other as to his All that he gives himself. We are, of course, speaking of the most successful human marriage relations and not of the failures; these latter remain all too possible, especially for lack of the ability to love in such a manner.

This other-centered love is not without the radical reference to self that is the mark of every natural human love to the extent that it is not elevated by and brought under the complete and perfect dominion of grace. If one finds his All in another, this is still in the other as another self (and therefore finally as somehow good-for the self). This follows from the metaphysical structure of natural human love. But at the same time, the metaphysical structure of natural sexual love, focusing on the other as fully another self—even as a part of one's integral being—also makes it to be the most fully other-centered mode of natural human love. Sexual intercourse is of itself expressive of this complete other-centeredness, of total personal giving in mutual communion. Such a love as this could clearly be only for *one* other at once.

When such a perfect sexual love is elevated by supernatural grace, it retains the same basic characteristic—that each person is All to the other. But supernatural charity, as we have seen, gives a new further orientation and drive towards God and towards a fullness of communion with God. Some day the "love unto folly" of married persons must end, at least in eternity; for charity must fructify into complete loving communion with God now present in vision. Then he will truly become the All for everyone who is with him. Rejoicing together in our supernatural friendship of charity, we will all see and love the Three who are much more than our friends, who are our All, whatever else they may have besides.

But even in this present life here below it is possible for men to arrive at a perfection of supernatural love of God that is in some ways parallel to the perfection of natural (and supernaturally elevated by grace) love in most successful marriages. This would be a "mystical love." As a mode of "love unto folly" it would be simply incompatible with the simultaneous presence of another such love. Only one other could be one's All at one time.

Yet this love inspired by supernatural grace would not be a love for God only as "another self" (such as would be any mere natural love, with its radical reference to the self), but even for God as the transcendent and infinite Self, good-for himself and also to and for his shared life of supernatural grace. The focal point of grace-inspired love is altogether outside oneself, even in the most radical sense. Such a love is never found isolated in the pure state in our present mode of being; there is also a (in itself neither sinful nor disorderly) natural element—a natural love—with it that retains an independent and radical reference to one-self in focusing upon what is good-for oneself. This element will, of course, remain even in eternal life with God; but there it will be completely integrated under the dominion of supernatural life. Our progress in supernatural life here below consists in large part in the growth of this dominion of supernatural grace even at present. In "mystical love" for God, the supernatural aspect clearly becomes more and more dominant; it is even possible for complete integration of everything else under the supernatural life to be achieved in the state of transforming union and the mystical light.

We need not carry this intricate and refined analysis any further, since what is of interest here is a more descriptive account of the supernatural mode of "love unto folly." In and through such a love of man for God, God shows himself more openly and enters into a more profound intimacy with the human spirit. In this love the real finality of supernatural grace in us emerges more into the light (though still in the obscurity of faith)—its tendency being towards the complete dominion of God in the soul, as the center of every activity, through supernatural faith, hope, and charity.

This supernatural mode of "love unto folly" is ultimately incompatible with another such simultaneous love in the order of human sexual relation, and indeed utterly transcendent in relation to such a sexual love in any event. There is, therefore, no possibility of analogizing from such a sexual human love in order to achieve an adequate reflex articulation of "mystical love" in thought or in particular day-to-day action. Passive contemplation, without the possibility of adequate active articulation, must begin here; this is a way of renunciation of means and a way of darkness for the spirit—in which it must be led by the Spirit rather than find its own way. Every articulation in terms of earlier experience is now simply insufficient to express what is now felt, and no acts are in any way adequate to testify to the true intensity of this love. Only silence, and perhaps also the most intense apostolic activity, come anywhere near expressing this personal devotion and intensity of affective communion with God and with Christ; and yet finally everything falls short.

There are no patterns in human love available here, except those we find in the revelation of God—especially in Scripture—in the life of Christ, and in the lives of the saints. But each one who follows this way must follow it in his own unique manner, under the guidance of God. Still, it is not true to say that the earlier modes of expressing friendship with God in articulated thought and action are simply dispensed with—far from it. Common morality always remains to be lived as perfectly as possible. Frequent articulated prayer goes right along with mystical prayer —articulation first in the liturgy of the Church but also in personal prayer outside the liturgical events. And as we have said, the modes of apostolic action still remain, perhaps now expanded both in variety and in scope.

So also, it remains true always that many human interpersonal relations of the most profound affective nature will help to deepen awareness and understanding, aid in greater reflex articulation, and also contribute to inventiveness in apostolic action— as well as enabling one better to carry out the simple exigencies of that fundamental love of neighbor that goes along with any friendship, and *a fortiori* such a friendship, with God and with Christ.

141

Only one such human interpersonal relation is excluded as incompatible with such a full love-relation to God; this is the "love unto folly" that ordinarily should mark successful marriage. And yet marriage itself is not excluded here. Neither is sexual intercourse within marriage (though it is deprived of its full symbolism of *complete* mutual giving of self—how could one give himself wholly to two Alls?). Perhaps the true "love unto folly" that is "mystical love" is not ordinarily found in such cases; but who could collect and offer statistics in this matter? In any event, this kind of supernatural "love unto folly" for God does mean that a union in marriage between "mystics" would have to be something less in itself than it would be if it were itself a "love unto folly" for these same persons. Of itself and apart from the consideration of special circumstances, perfect chastity would ordinarily be the "easier" way, freer of tension, for those who would wish to give themselves in such a manner to God. In this sense, chastity and the whole way of the counsels could be called the "ordinary way" of pursuing such a path of love of God.

In the light of these considerations, the supernaturally motivated renunciation of marriage, of sexual intercourse, of sexual pleasure, is of itself a preparation (negative, or even positive) in the supernatural order for such a higher mode of love of God. This renunciation is such a preparation precisely insofar as it excludes the other mode of "love unto folly" that could only exist among married persons and that would incarnate and symbolize itself in sexual intercourse. This renunciation is not of itself already the actual "achievement" (if we may so speak of what can only be a gift of God) of a "mystical" love of God; but it cannot help but point towards and even call for such a relation to God. The whole life of the evangelical counsels tends towards this ex-

142

clusive love of God that goes beyond mere friendship; and this kind of love of God does not seem really possible without something at least *equivalent* to what is ordinarily understood as the life of the counsels.

The renunciation of sexual love that is called for by the life of the counsels, and by evangelical chastity in particular, is of necessity more than just a renunciation of marriage and sexual intercourse. It requires also the renunciation of a large number of other intersexual relations that ultimately tend towards the full relation of marriage and intercourse, and that would consequently endanger this ideal of chastity. But at the same time, many other modes of human interpersonal relation through affective regard and communion are not only open to but are even very necessary for anyone who would preserve and grow in such an intense loving relation to God. Our love for family, friends, brothers or sisters in a religious community, or in some instances perhaps for a wife, contributes in several important ways towards the full expansion and development of that love "unto folly" of God that still transcends them all. We will now briefly dwell upon these ways.

As we have already pointed out, such well-ordered relations of love towards and communion with other human beings are analogues of human love for God. Even when there is question of "mystical love" for God, these analogues still help to deepen and support our partial and inadequate understanding of this relation to God and aid the ever inadequate articulation of our attitude in prayer. Such a "climate of human love," also elevated by supernatural grace, greatly facilitates those particular acts in relation to our neighbors towards which charity impels us. Even a natural love of others, comparatively uninfluenced by the life

143

of grace in us, could be a basis on which charity could build—though it could also be an obstacle to real supernatural charity if it tenaciously resists the dominion of charity.

Also, human love of the kind we are describing can remove very serious psychological obstacles that might otherwise be present, obstacles to the full appreciation and articulation, so far as possible, of our own love for God and for our neighbor, and also obstacles to the full appreciation, so far as possible, of God's own tender love and care for us. If we had no feeling of being loved by anyone, how could we really appreciate in our human way, however inadequate, God's love for us? How could we really articulate a love for God, whom we do not see, if we cannot feel profound affective regard for other human beings, whom we can see, or if we cannot articulate such a love for other human beings and express it in our various actions in their regard? We need both the experience of being loved by other human beings and that of loving them if we are to be able to live any kind of articulated supernatural life that is expressed in particular acts of love and care for both God and man.

It would, of course, be imprudent and even naïve not to take account of the very real dangers to supernatural life that human love of this kind can create. It would be quite possible for one to grow in attachment to friends so much that such friends come to stand alongside or even above God in the affections. It would be possible for one to fall gradually even into serious sexual difficulties. The varieties of human temperament make it necessary that no one simple standard of behavior be required of or imposed upon all in regard to human friendships. But we must always keep a sense of perspective, an awareness that a certain amount of possible and remote danger should be tolerated in view of the greater good of full human development and fuller relation with God. In fact, our life of human love is very important indeed in our religious life—and ordinarily all the more so in those who follow the way of religious chastity. It would be disastrous for the personality if some distorted ideal of religious detachment were to succeed in crippling or killing our capacity for human love of other human beings.

There is a certain amount of conventional nonsense regarding the saints. It is possible that some of them had no real human friendships; but the lives of the saints in general are full of examples of warm friendships, of saints surrounded even by a multitude of friends. Always they look towards a transcending of all such relations in their intense communion with God, but the richness and effectiveness of their human personalities in great part depends upon their capacity for human love. A chastity that would destroy this capacity would make one much less than he was, and would ratify the words of Piers Plowman, that "Chastity without charity will be chained in hell."

But it must finally be understood that religious chastity does fundamentally orient the human person towards a love of God that goes beyond all other loves and is a true "love unto folly." Chastity, of all the counsels, points out most vividly the radically mystical purpose of these counsels. If we have here emphasized the role of religious chastity as a preparation and disposition for a greater fullness of our affective love for God and man, this same chastity also has a very great value as regards the effective apostolate that should spring from such love, in all who are not living in a purely contemplative state. Let us now consider some of the more important aspects of the apostolic significance of religious chastity.

145

Religious chastity is of itself a sign of the eschatological kingdom already here present through grace. It bears witness to the
day when we shall all come to the fullness of supernatural life
with God in which there will be no marriage or giving in marriage. It also bears witness to the power of grace even here below.
Such a witness to the reality and primacy of the spiritual and
supernatural life of love of God has its powerful impact in the
world. In excluding the bond of married love, religious chastity
frees one for the concerns of God, for a really universal apostolate
in the love and service of all men. It gives a much clearer vision
of both material and spiritual reality, by freeing one from absorption in and centering on the pleasures and partnership of
sexual love.

If chastity has been insufficiently appreciated in recent years for
its apostolic power, as well as for its role in communion with
God, it nevertheless lacks nothing of its perennial value. It is only
necessary that we come to an adequate appreciation of the more
profound understanding of chastity and the requirements for successful living of such an ideal. Such adequate appreciation will
not lead to the abandonment of the ideal of religious chastity but
to an even greater perfection in its practice today.

There are many safeguards to religious chastity that are dic-
tated in large part by common sense. Clearly, these must still be
learned and preserved, today as much as ever, not only in the
course of education of new members of religious communities
but later as well. It is unnecessary here to enter into the details
of such a program. Only naïveté could question the reasons for
segregation of sexes and restrictions surrounding regarding the
living of the counsel of chastity. The same is to be said as regards

a somewhat larger area in which Christian modesty would have to be exercised, larger than that for those in or tending towards the married state.

But there must be adequate education for recognition of the real complementarity and mutually enriching role of the sexes in human life, for understanding their fundamental equality as well as their differing psychologies. It is impossible today to carry on with modern youth and young religious a successful program of sex education that would not meet their more sophisticated desire for fuller understanding of themselves precisely as masculine or feminine and therefore as naturally related to their complement. This is no matter of simple education to the simple physical sexual structures and functions. What is needed is much more— a real understanding of the proper psychological mystery of the other sex as well as of one's own. If such an understanding is absent, there is a felt ignorance of life that can only cause many more and serious problems. Without such an understanding, one is less a man or less a woman.

Such a more elaborate "sex education" of novices and young religious must of course be conducted only in the context of a presentation of the real meaning of the sacrifice entailed by religious chastity. This sacrifice must be seen not simply as a privation endured for the sake of an ascetical "test"—to prove one's strength of character—but in its direction towards fuller union and communion with God in "love unto folly" and towards total dedication to apostolic concern.

But once the meaning of chastity as directed towards greater love is seen, then the role here even of human love and friendship must be pointed out. The values of human friendship—for fuller spiritual life, for fuller human maturity, for better meeting

147

of human problems—must be opposed sharply to the concept of an "isolation with God" that would perhaps more commonly tend towards a rather narcissistic preoccupation with oneself and one's subjective states.

We must beware of pseudo-idealizations of the saints, and of the rhetorical exaggerations of ascetical writers. The saints too had need of human friendship. Human love enriched their lives just as it does ours. If we are to grow in our human capacity for love and the expression of love—the capacity that is supposed for the actual articulation and day-to-day manifestation of our supernatural love for God and for our neighbor—then we must have the experience of this love. Nor would it be enough to have this experience only as a past recollection from earlier life in the family circle and in the world. One can dry up, and forget how to love in a human way, unless this capacity is renewed, stirred to new growth, by the continuing interpersonal involvement of human friendship.

In this regard it is well to approach with a somewhat lighter touch the problem of the so-called "particular friendship" that has so much preoccupied many spiritual directors of the past. There is a genuine problem here. There is question of an immature affective relationship that is far too much under the domination of an emotion that goes beyond all bounds. Such relations must finally be controlled or cut off. But at the same time, we must not allow ourselves to be stampeded through fear or excessive caution into looking for the simple removal of emotion and warmth from human friendship. This would be to aim at the ideal of a rather mechanical man or woman, perhaps really incapable of any profound human love. Such a person would be "immature" in the sense that he or she was not allowed ever to grow to the full capacity for human affective relation to other human beings. Such a person would perhaps have some serious deficiency in dealing with other persons in the work of the apostolate, and might find a relative impoverishment in his or her life of prayer and communion with God.

Yet human love does have different characteristics in persons of different temperaments. Some are much more affective than others; some put much more emphasis upon practical and effective love that really does do, more than feel, good for other persons. Again it is impossible to set down any kind of uniform norms for such things. But the general implications of all that has been said are clear enough, it seems.

Chastity always remains the model for every form of Christian religious chastity. Christ had, of course, the highest degree of "love unto folly" for his heavenly Father, and consequently for his Father's will. It is in this light that we should look upon his frequent resort to prayer in solitude. His Father was his All, here on earth just as in eternity. The chastity of Christ was therefore most congruous with his inner communion with God in the depth of his human heart. But in this union and communion with his Father, and flowing out of this very union and communion, he showed the most complete and tenderest love for all men, and especially for his very own. A reading of John 13–17 would far surpass any words that could be added here to demonstrate this fact. We see this tender love again when we look at him, just a few days earlier, weeping over the death of Lazarus, or at another time weeping over the city of Jerusalem. He was not the kind of mystic so totally absorbed in the One, or in the "divine darkness," or even in the "divine light," that he had no love to give and to manifest openly to his fellow men. Rather, he radiated this love to all around him, and especially to his very own. This love of Christ must be our own exemplar that guides our effort (aided by grace) just as it guides his own hand in drawing us to himself and making us true instruments of his peace.

VI.

CONTEMPLATION IN ACTION

THE purpose of this chapter is twofold. It seeks first for an understanding of the role of the traditional "two ways" of contemplative prayer in the light of an underlying unity running throughout our relationship to God in prayer. Such an understanding becomes possible through a metaphysical analysis of prayer in its most fundamental aspect, as interpersonal communion with God through our affective regard for him. Then we shall try to broaden the idea of contemplative prayer through a further analysis, again metaphysical, of the structure of contemplation in action.

In the history of spiritual theology, two fundamentally different approaches to that higher form of communion with God called "contemplation" have taken form. On the one hand is the more common approach of the Greek Fathers that was taken also by the spiritual writers of the earlier Middle Ages, capsulized in the formula: reading, meditation, prayer, contemplation. On the other hand is the "negative theology" of Pseudo-Denis, especially taken up by the fourteenth-century mystics like

151

Eckhart, Tauler, Suso, Ruysbroeck, Hilton, and the author of *The Cloud of Unknowing,* and later followed up by John of the Cross and, to a certain extent, Teresa of Avila.

The former approach might be characterized as proceeding by way of a "positive theology," by an intense and thorough use of such images and concepts and formulations of every kind as might be available in Christian tradition. But the latter approach urges the Christian to leave all these things behind, in order to encounter God himself, who utterly transcends any finite formulation of whatever kind, and consequently cannot ever be encompassed or captured in himself in any way or to the slightest degree by such formulations. God is here seen as a darkness, a Nothing, in relation to all such formulations.

In the former way, the love of God is stirred by a consideration of the finite forms and beings that reflect to us in their finite way his own infinite being. This stirring, of course, presupposes that the consideration is made in the light of divine faith; and it leads to acts of supernatural charity, to the love of God above all things. But in the latter way there is no need of much consideration of finite things or of the formulations we make of what we know in finite ways. Rather, here the love of God arises immediately out of a very intense habit of charity in one who clings to God in pure faith in darkness and obscurity.

The common interpretation, for many centuries, of this distinction between the two approaches has been to make a sharp break between two ways or paths, corresponding to two quite distinct levels of spiritual life or two stages. Thus we distinguish between the ordinary, common way and that of infused contemplation. But the distinction is in fact difficult to sustain.

In the first place, before the Pseudo-Denis, and also afterwards well into the Middle Ages, and indeed right on up to the present, it was and is possible to follow the first way and end in a contemplation that is indistinguishable from that of the second way. Also, it is generally admitted that genuinely infused contemplation would be in itself a gift that would not really *flow* from the practice of any methods, whether of positive or of negative theology. And if we distinguish between the theory of positive and negative theology and the actual living and prayer that fit such theory, we must acknowledge that both modes of living and prayer tend towards a supernatural love which is at the same time also communion with God, a communion that in itself simply transcends any finite formulations and any theories. The orthodox mystics themselves, despite their metaphor and hyperbole, have always emphasized the continuity of their prayer with the essential life of loving faith that is found in all good Christians; the presence of God to them is only a further growth of this life of loving faith. The growing tendency today is to emphasize the fundamental continuity of the life of prayer, with the ascetical and mystical elements viewed as complementary at every stage and not merely as successive. If there is a "special" way of high contemplation, in this view it would not be the result of a radically different mode of spiritual life but rather of a further stage of growth that is simply not reached by the greater number.

What is essential and important in each of the two ways is that one comes to the very presence of God as known in faith and loved in charity. If it has been sometimes possible to distinguish between a prayer that is only a set of acts, concepts, propositions, images, and methods, and another prayer that is genuine communion with the present God, this could only have been done because the finality of the first type of prayer was lost sight of. But it may be hoped that the practice of such prayer was much more successful than its theory, and that it too actually has led many souls to the very presence of God through faith and love. In any event, it is now possible to take a much more satisfactory view of the "two ways" of prayer.

If we consider the essence of the spiritual life as an interpersonal relationship with God and with Christ, it is possible to conceive such a difference as we have noted in modes of prayer as simply a function of the various stages through which such interpersonal relation to God and Christ passes. But before attempting to treat the possibility and nature of such stages and degrees of this relation, it is well for us to consider briefly the nature of the relation itself. This will force us to touch, still lightly however, on some metaphysical considerations.

In recent years, many philosophers have come to distinguish from the merely objective and objectifying mode of knowledge, characteristic of any science, that more intimate union that can be found in poetic intuition or in profound human friendship. Such a distinction between objective and objectified presence on the one hand and "intersubjective" presence on the other seems a sufficiently established fact, indeed a primary datum of experience, to many reflective modern men. If it is still denied by some, those who are more aware of it cannot help but feel very much like the Aristotelian or Thomist who hears positivists deny the reality of his knowledge of transphenomenal natures in reality. The distinction is, in any case, assumed in all that follows in this chapter.

But such a phenomenological distinction between two radically different modes of presence of the other to the knower also calls for some deeper explanation. Nor would it be sufficient simply to posit some new mode of intellectual intuition—something like the physical *vis* that can be postulated to explain any new physical effect. Such a hypothetical new mode of intellectual intuition would have to be explained in detail, so that one could understand with some degree of clarity how it is that this "intersubjective" presence does not always arise with the same degree of intensity, that it seems to be only rather minimal in cases in which there is no profound affective commitment or regard for the person or thing that is known, that it does arise as something *more*—above and beyond the concomitant objective presence of "ordinary knowledge."

Without entering into a full discussion here of this insufficiency of any purely intellectual intuition to account for the characteristics of intersubjective presence in its more intense forms, in poetic experience and in human friendship, we can find a more adequate explanation in the metaphysical structure of human spiritual love. Such love in fact includes a reference to the subjectivity of that which is loved. By "subjectivity" we here mean that incommunicable root in a being of the unique exercise of existence and activity which are proper to this being and to no other. (Thus we are not speaking of the notion of subjectivity in much of contemporary philosophy that refers only to the inward being of conscious persons, but of a fundamentally Thomist notion that is verified of every being that exists fully in its own right.) When this "subjectivity" is the subjectivity of a being that is intellectually self-conscious and free, then it becomes the personality of a person. Through love we enter into relation not just to our knowledge of persons or things but to the things themselves, and not just to some one or other of the objective facets of things but to the very subjectivity of the thing and to

155

the very heart of personality in the person. Moreover, this love is a conscious act, because of its spirituality and because of the presence of the intellect and will in each other. But the intellectual consciousness of love is necessarily also a consciousness of the reference that has just been pointed out of this love to the subjectivity of the loved. This consciousness of subjectivity as the focus of affective regard is a characteristically new mode of consciousness, a consciousness of intersubjective, and interpersonal, relation that is quite distinct from ordinary objective intellectual knowledge and also from a minimal intersubjective presence of the other that does in fact arise along with any such objective intellectual knowledge.

It is possible to make a deeper analysis of the metaphysical structure of this mode of consciousness,[1] but here it is enough merely to note its presence. The intellect is here conscious through the formal medium of love, and in some manner enters into union with the very subjective depth, the incommunicable otherness, of the other who is loved.

Such a mode of intersubjective presence is also found in a minimal degree in every instance of our knowledge of things, in virtue of the spontaneous passion of love that is induced in the will by such knowledge. But it can rise to a great degree of intensity when this spontaneous passion is followed by intense freely given regard and commitment. It is possible for such regard and commitment to range even beyond what is here and now present, to persons or things that are physically absent from the knower, and to give rise to this intersubjective presence of the

[1] See our *Inquiry Into Being,* Chicago, Loyola University Press, 1965, pp. 150–154; and *The Christian Intellect and the Mystery of Being,* The Hague, Martinus Nijhoff, 1966, Chapter VI.

loved even in the physical absence of the loved. But there is a much fuller, more concrete mode of this presence when the loved is actually physically present.

Further, if God can be said to be in some manner absent, by reason of his utter transcendence, he is also present in us by his grace; and through charity we can enter his heart. Thus such an intersubjective, interpersonal presence as we have described— of God to us, as well as of us to God—is in an obscure manner constitutive in varying degrees throughout our life of grace. Every mode of supernatural, grace-inspired affective regard for God gives rise to a very obscure, but still fundamentally conscious, union with God, but a union that is simply outside of purely objective categories and that rises to full communion when this affective regard becomes a genuine charity which regards God as *the* good above all else, to whom one gives his whole life.

It is possible to speak of the spiritual life of man with God in terms of the objective structures discerned both in man and in our knowledge of God by ontological analysis in the light of faith. It is also possible to dwell upon the various psychological states that may be met with in the course of this spiritual life. And there is a more practical approach to spiritual life that will offer guidance to the soul on the way to God. But it also seems possible to make another kind of ontological analysis, this time of the intersubjective structure of our life with God, of the inter-personal relation that is surely the fundamental point of the life of grace. Such a mode of analysis should be closely linked with the ontological analysis of objective structure, since in fact these are not separate. As Maritain says, objects are only aspects of subjects. But it does not seem necessary for us to repeat here what has already been said in enough treatises of dogmatic, ascetical, and mystical theology concerning the objective structure of the various principles of spiritual life. Rather, we shall attend directly to the intersubjective structure, trying to understand something of the ontological basis for various modes of prayer. This is only right, for supernaturally inspired prayer is of its nature an inter-subjective reality, a relation of, a communion between, subject and Subject.

If prayer is such an interpersonal communion, it should be possible to gain some better understanding of it in comparing it to more ordinary human interpersonal relations such as friend-ship. We notice that such a human relationship is ordinarily not given in full bloom all at once, but that it is rather the result of a long growth. The first encounter is of course already an inter-personal relation, but not yet one which really takes hold firmly of the persons involved. But more than passing interest is stirred, and a long process of free and deeper entry into fuller com-munion begins.

In the earlier stages of this movement towards "heart-to-heart" communion there is more concern for external behavior on both sides. Here each one must act rather tentatively, and note care-fully the response from the other. Gradually the assurance of genuine mutual interest and regard grows upon both, and a sense of secure mutual acceptance permeates the relation. This sense of acceptance and assurance of being loved does not arise merely from the whole pattern of objective signs in speech and other forms of behavior, but more fundamentally from one's own love for the other. For this love, now much more intense than before, is a formal medium of union with the very depth of subjectivity—the heart—of the other. If the various objective signs are indeed necessary conditions for this love and inter-subjectivity, this latter is still something quite different; the security, assurance, and sense of acceptance are not the result of some logical deduction but flow from a "logic of the heart." And yet this is not to say that there is no objective ground for it; the objective signs have indeed been given by the other that such an affective commitment is both warranted and reciprocated. It is just that we simply transcend all the evidence of such signs in the higher and deeper knowing that flows from love itself.

But if the objective signs have been so very necessary as a support for the deep commitment that gives rise to such a more intense interpersonal communion grounded in love, this also means that the signs have preoccupied the mind and the attention —the actual union of hearts has been growing, but as a kind of background against which the continuing concern for the objective signs is the really dominant psychological factor. In some manner the relation still lives on and feeds from the little objective signs and tokens of deeper love. Were they withdrawn, because of mutual absence or any other reason, the interpersonal communion would itself gradually diminish so that all that was gained would gradually be lost again.

Yet it is possible for friendship to grow far beyond this point, so that regard for so many little external details simply gives way to utter immersion in real heart-to-heart communion. There will still be signs and tokens of love, but now they do not so much nourish love as themselves flow from this communion. Indeed, they are no longer necessary to sustain it; neither absence, nor sickness, nor misunderstanding, nor even death itself can destroy the roots of such love. Mutual trust, and an understanding that

159

transcends all misunderstandings, result in loyalty and fidelity stronger than death. We see this trust and fidelity in the most successful and happy marriages and in the most outstanding examples of human friendship. One is fortunate indeed to have found one such human relationship in his life.

Of course, a relationship of this kind does not just happen. It ordinarily results from prolonged growth in love, that could only take place in persons who have both a capacity to love and a responsiveness to signs that at least in this case go far beyond what we ordinarily show in our daily living. Attentiveness and the taking of pains must mark the earlier phases. Perseverance despite temporary difficulties and minor differences, and even through crises, is only expected. Such love as this has a great price; the greatest human lovers pay it cheerfully, unless the suffering is too intense—but then they still pay it. Through such pains, difficulties, and crises, friends and lovers come to deeper communion of spirit than ever before or perhaps than ever would have been possible for them otherwise.

When we turn to consider our supernatural life of interpersonal relation with God, and those special periods in it that we call "formal prayer," it is well to bear in mind the context in which it exists. There is in fact a prior natural presence of God in the depth of the soul, an obscure intersubjective presence that is concomitant with and at the very ground of all the rest of our conscious life. But this is not all. In every movement of our spirit, in all its intellectual life of knowing and loving, there is also given again in a concomitant intersubjectivity the presence of God as the source that gives being to and sustains this intellectual life. God is thus never really absent from our consciousness, but this kind of presence is in itself thoroughly obscure and unformulated and not susceptible of direct formulation and reflex consciousness. Yet, obscure as it is, this presence is already constitutive of a fundamental attitude of the created person, open in virtue of his very being and activity to the presence of God. If God should somehow speak to such a created person, this would not be an intrusion into his privacy but a word to one already constituted as listener and hearer in the very structure of his consciousness.

There is also a more discursive approach to God, still in itself natural (though our nature is not left alone to follow it without the solicitations of grace). By this way we can become more explicitly aware, and in a formulated manner of knowing, of this divine presence both to us and to all that is. But this discursive way, simple in itself and to the spontaneous and global knowledge of common sense, is difficult to trace out reflectively in detail unless one is a metaphysician—and even then it is difficult.

We have not been left to make our way to God, or to be led by him to himself, by the tortuous way of natural reason alone. Grace and revelation are offered to all men. Grace and revelation solicit all men from the very dawn of their moral life in the attraction that they feel towards the full totality of the moral order, in a solicitation for an unqualified basic moral option for the universal moral good. More especially, this working of grace and revelation gradually emerges into the light, as the grace of Christ, through the progressive historical self-revelation of God that culminates in the coming of Christ, and in his foundation of the Church. Our consideration in what follows focuses upon the Christian situation, which is the highest moment and fullness of this divine self-revelation.

Christian life and Christian prayer are a supernatural encounter with God and with Christ in the context of supernatural faith, hope, and charity (unless charity, and perhaps even hope, were absent because of sin). From the very outset, this encounter means a special interpersonal presence of God, as we have seen, in virtue of the very structure of supernatural affective regard for God. In everyone who has supernatural charity, this inter-personal presence of God even deserves the name of the divine indwelling. Prayer is not really distinct from this life itself; but we use the term *prayer* to describe those moments or periods in which we in some manner, directly or obliquely, focus our attention as much as we can on this divine presence—this is formal prayer.

But if personal regard in loving communion through charity is what matters most in Christian life and prayer, this is not ordinarily so clearly apprehended at first. What at first preoc-cupies the attention of the ordinary Christian is the testimony of God's revelation that is offered to the Christian through the Church. He considers the articles of faith, the symbolic forms of worship, the commandments of God, and the precepts of au-thority in the Church. He hears the testimony of divine love in a formulated message, in which he also finds given a pattern of what is expected from him by way of response. "If you love me, keep my commandments." In this state he can begin and carry through, with the help of divine grace, that "reform of faith" which is expected of every Christian. But though he hears the call to love, still he can only understand this call in a rather minimal manner. There is in fact genuine love and personal regard; but the foreground of consciousness is absorbed rather in forms and formulations that are ultimately the work of, but nevertheless *are not,* God. Prayer at this point is a set of partic-

162

ular acts, practices, chains of reflection, meditation. These are some of the objective signs and tokens of love (to which all our good works must be added) that are, with the help of grace, shown by us to God as a kind of response to what we have heard and believed concerning all the saving acts of God in human history. These saving acts of God are the objective signs and tokens of love on his side. The situation is very similar to that of the earlier phase of human friendship that we described above.

At this point in Christian life there can and ought finally to come (were it not for maladies of body and mind that can obscure it beyond our recognition frequently enough) a sense of security, assurance, and acceptance by God that flows from our own love for him and our intersubjective communion, in virtue of this love, with him. Again, this "logic of the heart" is not really ungrounded; it is grounded in the very real objective signs that God has given in history, and perhaps also in our personal lives, of his love for us. But again we transcend all the evidence of such signs in the higher and deeper knowing that flows from our supernatural love itself. (Yet this knowing is not susceptible of clear and certain reflex formulation—but is this not so even of ordinary human love of friendship?)

Still, this interpersonal communion with God and with Christ, though more intense, draws much support from those objective signs of God's love for us and from the signs that the grace of God draws forth from us in response. Without these signs our faith, hope, and love would be most severely tried; without them our whole supernatural life would very likely wither and die, except perhaps in its most radical depth.

In order that one can progress further in heart-to-heart communion with God, even to the point of utter immersion in God himself in a love that is now able to disregard all the scaffolding of signs and simply come to immediate rest in God, some kind of weaning from our dependence on all these signs and tokens is necessary. It is at this point that one comes to the classical mystic way (though of course God could accomplish the same result in some other more immediate way, if he so chose to do). But this weaning process must not be misunderstood. Its purpose is that one might adhere more firmly to God by a more purified faith, hope, and love. It is not that one might eventually be able to transcend even supernatural faith.

Faith itself has two aspects: that of intersubjective union with God, which is perfected further through hope and becomes true communion through charity; and that of articulation in the propositions, symbolic forms, legislation, and structural character of the Church. But the Christian adheres to both; the more deeply he enters into intersubjective communion with God, the more firmly he holds to the articulations that are themselves also finally from God. These articulations always lead him back to God. And if he enters into periods, even if prolonged, of simple inarticulate rest in God, this itself can only be due to his believing adherence in living hope and love to the uncreated speech of God. Words are not necessary for him at this moment, not because he no longer believes but because of the very intensity of his belief and love. So it is that he will always humbly submit any account he might give of such states to the judgment of the Church.

However, the purification of prayer must be accomplished in some manner, if one is to learn eventually to attend to the very presence of the uncreated and infinite God alone, with his love,

164

and not be distracted by the consideration of finite forms and formulations. It is true that these could very well lead one to the point at which he virtually falls into such a presence of God (but always drawn by a special grace of love); but they could just as well bind one down to them, so that God himself would be encountered only in a relatively oblique manner.

The modes in which such a purification of prayer can take place are limitless in number. There is, of course, a certain simplification of prayer that is itself natural, the result of a psychological law. Meditative consideration of the truths of God through many acts of knowledge and love gradually tends to take place more easily in fewer discrete acts, even up to the point of reaching the prayer of simplicity. But even this natural psychological process makes its own contribution to the gradual movement of the focus of attention from the multiplicity of objective signs and tokens to the one presence of the revealing and loving God. Something similar must be said of the gradual decline of attraction for illicit creatures and manners of action, though this process of detachment must eventually lead beyond to complete detachment from every creature of any kind except insofar as it is willed for us by God.

There must finally be such detachment from all images, emotions, concepts, judgments, and the joy that arises from them, if one is to encounter God in pure faith and love. Utter aridity of spirit, crises and sufferings of every kind, may be necessary to this end. God's seeming absence, and even the decline into seeming insignificance of every one of the signs that were once held dear, may be needed as means to fuller growth in real love (and therefore in real, however masked for the time being, interpersonal communion with God). All the rest is unimportant;

165

God and his love alone matter. But clearly, such a growth in communion with God must of necessity be a growth in faith—it is at this point an entry into utter darkness, the divine darkness that can be illumination only for faith.

Through such a process one can move beyond the "reform in faith" to which all Christians are called, to the deeper "reform in feeling" where we no longer merely consider the exterior actions of Christ but even come to share his inner feelings. In thus "putting on Christ" we come to a higher level of contemplation in communion with Christ in a really heart-to-heart manner. We have a connaturality with Christ himself. This connaturality is not just a connaturality of charity but even of the entire organism of the virtues as informed by charity. Through it is understood, as through some kind of mirror, the very being of love, and so also the inner being of our Lord's human spiritual life. This reformed life of ours is truly a sharing in some limited manner in the supernatural life that our Lord possessed in a certain fullness. Such a contemplation of the inner dispositions of the Word in his humanity is contemplation of the Sacred Heart.

Our contemplation of Christ in his heart need not stop here. In the heart of Christ, in our connaturality with his heart, the very Godhead—Father, Son, and Holy Spirit—must also be encountered.

Is it thus further possible that interpersonal communion with God and with Christ could take on even a consciously Trinitarian form, in the manner described by John of the Cross? It does not appear that the ordinary dynamism of charity towards intersubjective, interpersonal communion with God could of itself come to such a term in immediate consciousness of the real processions themselves and of the real personal distinctions themselves.

If this term is in fact reached, there is need of some further "mystical light" which would illuminate in a new way what has been hitherto attained only in virtue of loving faith. Such a "mystical light" could change one's entire psychological focus, even to permitting awareness of the non-mediated presence of the Trinity, not to the intellect (as in the beatific vision) but to the will. Here there would be a radical transformation of consciousness, much more radical than anything that has gone before. We will not dwell any further on this transformation however—it is surely a mode of prayer, attested to by such mystics as John of the Cross and Ignatius of Loyola, but its utter transcendence must simply escape our view.

Yet even without the aid of such a mystical light, this interpersonal communion with the Godhead in faith and love is already understood, in the light of faith, as communion in fact with the Trinitarian God—there is no other God. Even apart from the mystical light this would be a great height of prayer and communion with God. In such a loving contemplation in faith of the Trinity in God, through connaturality with the heart of Christ, one could find a great peace that might no longer be touched by all the disturbances and troubles of daily life. But just as in very deep human friendship, such a friendship with God is ordinarily the result of long growth in the life of grace, growth that is "bought" only at the price of much suffering.

Our grace is always the grace of Christ, and always bears the imprint of the cross. Suffering and love are always entwined in our lives, even as regards merely human loves, but above all in the course of our growth in communion with God and with

Christ. We come to God through Christ, by a grace for which Christ himself is the exemplar. If this must be so for all men, it is more especially so for us Christians—but for us this is not merely an objective fact, but a mystery open to never-ending contemplation. So the cross even becomes the most fundamental symbol of the salvation in which we believe. But it is a cross that also looks towards and recalls to mind the resurrection.

In the light of the foregoing brief outline of growth in Christian life as interpersonal communion with God and with Christ, it is possible to make a few remarks concerning the traditional distinction between the "two ways" of prayer, one characterized by the use of finite forms and formulations as means and the other characterized by the flight from all such finite forms and formulations through a lived "negative theology." Two phases of prayer can indeed be distinguished in this manner, but such a distinction must be hedged with qualifications.

In the light of our understanding of spiritual life in terms of interpersonal relationship, we must note that the move from positive to negative theology (not in the purely theoretical order, but in the order of *lived* prayer) is not so much a *break* as a reasonable development. Much has been made of this transition in terms of the distinction between ordinary prayer and infused contemplation. But perhaps it might be better to reserve the phrase *infused contemplation* for only those states which are produced by the mystical light, rather than for every state in which negative theology is predominant.

In fact, negative theology begins quite early in spiritual life. The theory of it could, of course, be known to anyone, even to someone who does not pray at all. But its living in prayer can also begin quite early, through meditation upon the writings of mystics. (And yet this is not quite lived negative theology in the formal sense, since it is sustained by meditation on negative concepts rather than by a real flight from concepts and images.) One progresses in the direction of negative theology even in the prayer of simplicity, when the necessity for more complex discursive acts gives way to the possibility of simpler intuitive acts. This is even more so of affective prayer, and in the case of the profound peace of fleeting moments at the onset of the prayer of quiet. There is not yet any question of complete emancipation from finite forms and formulations, objective signs and tokens. But there is slowly dawning upon the soul in prayer the realization that the presence of God really does completely transcend all particular acts of knowing and loving. And yet the actual determination to resort to negative theology as to the fundamental "method" for formal prayer is still a matter in which greatest prudence should be exercised. What is needed is a readiness for simple communion with the divine presence, but coupled with a willingness to use the other way to the extent that such a simple communion in love does not arise in the soul.

Always the goal is to enter into a conscious interpersonal communion in love with God. We simply do what helps to bring us there, understanding that it is grace which must draw and lead us and that we can get nowhere by ourselves in this domain. In the more common case, images, concepts, formulas, techniques, and observances have their use in disposing us for the love that is the formal principle of such communion with God. But we must never forget that they are only dispositive. They could even lead us in the wrong direction, towards absorption in them and in our own states of consciousness—as our own—instead of towards loving attention to God. It is quite necessary to be looking beyond them from the very start, by an orientation towards God himself as simply transcending all methods and all finite forms. Even in purely speculative theology, St. Thomas Aquinas took care, almost at the beginning of the *Summa Theologiae* (I, q. 3, prol.), to emphasize the deeper truth of negative theology, before embarking on his detailed positive consideration of the divine attributes. Such an initial orientation could spare many persons from some degree of eventual disillusionment, or from something of agonizing anguish that may come when all the methods fail, and when finite forms leave one unstirred.

But if there are those who do finally come to a point at which their prayer is principally a lived negative theology, nevertheless there are others who continue to find great value in finite forms, images, and so forth, precisely as dispositions to a deeper affective communion with God himself. This may also be true, we may note, in many instances of human friendship. Particularly do women tend to require such signs and tokens of the underlying intersubjective communion. It is not that the love, connaturality, and interpersonal relationship are not ever intensifying. It is rather simply that for such persons, their sensibility continues to crave this objective correlate of loving communion. Pure negative theology is not what they want, and indeed it is not what they need. But what is important is that they always see beyond the objective signs to the presence of God.

In such a context it might be well to note the completely subsidiary place in the life of prayer, even in "mystical" prayer, occupied by such phenomena as visions, revelations, and peripheral sensible phenomena of all kinds. Such things might be of some manner of help to some and more of a distraction to others. Some of this phenomena might be genuinely of divine origin; but most of it no doubt results from the release of some energy in the subconscious domain, a release associated with psychical nervous tension. There is perhaps some harmony between these observations and the apparent fact that many people, especially women, do very much need, and indeed have, some more or less marked mode of resonance in sensibility even for the highest degrees of spiritually affective communion with God.

But always what matters is love, the fundamental love of charity that is the formal principle of Christian interpersonal communion with Christ and with the Trinity. This same charity is also the principle of supernatural interpersonal communion with our neighbor, and therefore also of any true Christian apostolate. All the rest in the Church exists for the sake of this love. All the rest in our personal lives as Christians must be for this love and from this love.

The full pattern of life and prayer is filled out by our own degree of this affective communion with God, our individual temperament, and our place in the world. Some things in this pattern are constant, or relatively so, for all Christians. Negative and positive morality, arising from the nature of man and of the world as well as from the laws and authority of both God and man, our continual existence as parts of a community under God, the impulse of charity towards some kind of apostolic concern for all men—all these are in general common to all Christians. But the individual concrete life of prayer differs greatly in different persons and at different times. Positive considerations of finite forms and objective signs may no longer play the same role as before. The infused mystical light may even radically alter the mode of consciousness of God. Long before this change takes place, however, a more negative and passive approach may begin to appear and gradually to dominate in our interpersonal communion with God.

But the interpersonal communion itself, through faith and love, has been all along from the very start in every case the very heart of Christian spiritual life and prayer. It is only a question of the mode in which one comes to this same communion and of the depth to which one becomes more directly aware of it. This does not mean that "mystical" prayer and the "mystic way" have been somehow degraded. Rather, it means that the mystical mode of interpersonal communion in fact extends backward into the spiritual life, even to its very beginnings. In ordinary Christian prayer, in one who loves God, there is already genuine interpersonal communion of this kind. Indeed, even in one who merely believes (and probably also hopes) in God, but with the absence of supernatural love that results from mortal sin, there can still be a prayer that attains some degree of interpersonal union (though not the fullness of communion). This is the ordinary case, so long as one is aiming to communicate with God himself, and not just to engage in some kind of mere play of images and concepts. We need not fear that God has eluded us in our prayer simply because all our images, concepts, and other such apparatus fall hopelessly far below his being. In affective regard for God, supernaturally inspired by grace, one simply transcends the limitations of all such creatures and is drawn into the personal presence of the infinite Lord.

We alluded above to differences in temperament among Christians, yet so far in our treatment of prayer we have attended only to those Christians who give much time to formal prayer, and indeed only insofar as their prayer is formal prayer. But there is another kind of prayer altogether, a prayer that is true prayer even in the midst of action, some form or other of contemplation in action. It seems clear enough that there are such forms of prayer, through which persons of action—in and through their very action itself—come to a kind of contemplation of God, an interpersonal communion which is not unlike that of the more strictly contemplative way. We should like to understand the nature of such prayer, possibly its diverse modes, its presuppositions, and its relation to the various forms of contemplative prayer that we have previously described.

In order the better to consider the structure of a Christian "contemplation in action" it seems well—at the risk of some repetition—to draw a brief outline of some modes of presence that philosophy itself to some extent at least could discern, modes that might enter into the constitution of some form of contemplation in action.

Two of these modes have already been pointed out. There is a natural presence of God in the depth of the soul, "obscure intersubjective presence that is concomitant with and at the very ground of all the rest of our conscious life." This presence arises ultimately in virtue of the spirituality of our substantial existence, corresponding to the spirituality of the human soul itself. Such a spiritual existence is of itself *intentional,* referring even in a conscious manner to the pure existence that is its source in God. Thus, in the obscure consciousness that we have of the exercise of our own spiritual existence, we are simultaneously conscious in obscurity of the divine existence from which our own existence springs, of this divine existence as the exemplar of our finite existence. We have noted elsewhere the possibility of bringing this obscure perception more to the foreground of consciousness by techniques similar to those of the Indian "mystics." For us it remains ordinarily very much in the background of consciousness, even after our attention has been directed to it by a poet or a philosopher, or even a mystic. But it is there, nevertheless, as a context for and fundamental openness to other more accessible modes of conscious union and communion with God.

The second mode of presence is very closely related to the first. It is the presence of God to the human knower, no longer in virtue of the spirituality of the existence proper to the human soul, but in virtue of the spirituality of all its intellectual life of knowing and loving. Once again, this spiritual mode—not of existing but of acting—has an immediate intentional reference to the divine being that is the immediate source, as First Cause, of every slightest stir of activity in created being. The same divine presence that constitutes, and is at once the primary intersubjective term of, the being-in-openness that is created spirit and spiritual existence—this divine presence is again encountered, in virtue of a similar metaphysical structure, at the level of activity in the created spirit. Just as obscure as the first, just as incapable of direct formulation and reflex consciousness, this presence nevertheless is a given that re-emphasizes our fundamental openness to God, and even to his word.

A third mode of presence is found in every free action by the human person. This is a presence of the end that is sought as the final goal of such action. Such a presence, in itself, is to be sure a presence across a distance. But the very inclination towards an end, even towards an end that does not yet exist, is already some kind of anticipation of the being of the end itself. If this inclination in the human will is one that is inspired by supernatural grace, then in it there is already some obscure anticipation of the being of God himself, who is the ultimate goal of such a tendency.

Another mode of presence is closely related to the preceding one. If the inclination of the human will is towards some person or thing that indeed already exists, and is moreover perhaps already in some manner physically present to the one who loves it or tends towards it in this manner, then this inclination of the will becomes a formal medium through which a new mode of presence of what is loved arises even to the intellect. If this occurs under the inspiration of supernatural grace, there arises an obscure, but immediate, intersubjective, interpersonal presence of God. And if this inclination is in fact true charity, then this interpersonal presence of God goes beyond mere union to true indwelling and communion.

A final mode of presence that might shed some light upon the notion of a Christian "contemplation in action" is the presence of God in a more objective manner (insofar as God himself is in some manner "objectified" by the constructs through which we speak of him and think of him in our human science of natural and supernatural theology, and in the symbols that reason and faith can offer to us). But here we are thinking of this kind of "wisdom" not insofar as it offers to us such constructs to think and speak of God, but rather insofar as it enables us to see in its light that every creature is in its own unique manner a reflection, manifestation, and sign of the divine being—even a kind of "sacrament" of God. Such a perspective on creatures and on the whole of created being permits one who has arrived at this height of philosophical and/or theological wisdom to "find God in all things" in a rather literal sense. If all this should take place in one who has come also to a profound degree of interpersonal communion with God in supernatural charity, then perhaps there is in him a real fullness of contemplation in action.

We shall return to these modes of presence in an attempt to construct a synthetic notion of contemplation in action. Now, however, it may be useful to make a few remarks of a more historical nature concerning some actual notions of Christian contemplation in action.

It would be simply inaccurate to think that the ideal of contemplation in action is something characteristically modern, or at least not going back farther than the beginnings of the Society of Jesus. While it is true that the phrase "contemplative in action" seems to have been coined by the Jesuit Father Nadal in the sixteenth century, in fact the idea behind it can be found even in such a medieval treatise as *The Goad of Love* (a translation and retouching by Walter Hilton of a work falsely attributed to St. Bonaventure). There we can see very clearly the idea of a contemplation through love that in fact endures as the one possessing it goes out to activity. He is to come to such a degree of communion with Christ that he will continue to encounter him even after leaving off from formal prayer. Something similar is to be found in the early Christian monks, but of course it is also sought by serious Christians everywhere. What was new in the Society of Jesus was the conception that such action might range far beyond what would have been previously dreamed of, at least in the ordinary case of the devout person. Now it is thought to be possible really to "find God in all things," even in the midst of the greatest preoccupation with apostolic activity. There is also a further element—God is truly to be found *in* all things. This latter, especially, calls for our attention.

Generally, one can distinguish between two aspects of contemplation in action. There is first the necessity for familiarity with God in continuous formal prayer, which brings about a close union between such prayer and apostolic activity. In this kind of life one is strengthened and guided towards action by prayer and, on the other hand, urged to more prayer by this action itself.

This aspect of contemplation in action is in no way special; it has been a mark of apostolic men since the beginning of Christianity. But the second aspect is more specific and calls for further explanation. This aspect includes the Teilhardian encounter with God in the very depths of finite reality. We shall devote our attention in particular to this characteristic aspect of contemplation in action.

The contemplation here is not something parallel to the action, that happens to be sustained during the action or encouraged between actions, but is rather something that results precisely in virtue of the action itself. This must be kept in mind during our attempt to achieve a synthetic understanding of such a contemplation in action. It would not be enough to arrive at a notion of this contemplation that would only be an extension of a contemplation that arises simply in virtue of the metaphysical structure of charity that in an implicit, but nevertheless actual, manner continues to dominate and permeate our consciousness and action even in the midst of every kind of activity for the glory of God and the salvation of souls.

Yet such contemplation through charity (and of course through faith as well) is surely still a key element in this notion of contemplation in action. After all, if contemplation of God means the presence in a conscious manner of God, and indeed of God as *loved,* then this contemplation through charity is still at the heart of the matter. But contemplation *in action* adds something else. Contemplation in action adds some kind of new sight and love of the finite realities and acts with which one is concerned, in the light of a vision of faith. This vision of faith might vary in individuals, but in some manner or other it must be at least able to convey the Christian sense of the *sacramentality* of creatures in relation to God, that every creature does in fact have a sign-value according to which it is also a revelation of God, so that in its truth might be known and in its goodness might be tasted something of God's own truth and goodness. But before we proceed on this line let us first discuss the notion and structure of a supernatural encounter with God "in the depths of the finite."

Supernatural encounter with God in the depths of the finite other must of course have a metaphysical structure somewhat different from that of the simple interpersonal loving communion with God in the depth of the soul. Nor, if God is somehow truly encountered, "found," in the other, could this come about simply in virtue of the spiritual intentionality of one's own existence or intellectual activity. An awareness of God through such spiritual intentionality, besides being as obscure as it is, is also an awareness either through one's *own* being or through one's *own* operation, and consequently could not be described as encounter with God "in the finite other."

And yet such an unformulated and even unformulatable consciousness-in-the-dark, through the intentionality of the spiritual existence and activity of the human person, of a transcendent plenitude does in fact present God as the background of all things, as an infinite whole or "ocean of being" that contains all things in some super-eminent manner. But then everything else must refer to this fullness, as somehow a finite mode of this

178

infinite. Everything else, in all its essential and existential content of being, is also somehow precontained in and somehow something of God, the supreme unity of infinite being. Thus everything we see around us manifests something of God.

But in such a perception as this, through spiritual intentionality, still far below the level of formulating reflection and only capable of interpretation in the light of some such formulating reflection, nothing is yet seen clearly of the actual causal dependence of every existence upon the divine being. Such an obscure intuition could in fact very easily be misinterpreted as meaning a simple identity of the various finite modes with the infinite plenitude of being. And it would not be enough, it would even be dangerous, to attempt to conceptualize—in the light only of a common sense given to poetic and magical fantasies—this obscure intuitive content. Without the aid of a metaphysical or theological understanding and without the aid of a theory of analogy of being, or without at least the illumination of an articulated divine faith, it would be only too easy for such a person to fall into some form of pantheism or monism. Although the most outstanding examples of such an aberration are to be found in Indian thought, nevertheless the West has not lacked both poets and philosophers of this kind.

The more explicitly formulated approach of Christian philosophical and theological inquiry, or at least of the Christian faith, leads to a clearer understanding of the complete distinction and transcendence of God in relation to all finite being. At the same time it provides some understanding of the real presence of God in every creature, insofar as God is the first and immediate cause of every finite being. When there is such an understanding of the divine omnipresence, presence at the heart of the being of

179

every being, then it is possible for the intellect, especially as enlightened by faith, and above all as guided by a love of supernatural charity for God that really does seek him through and in
all things, to "find God in all things." Our original openness to
God in virtue of our being as spiritual and intellectual beings,
openness that is understood in a more formulated and explicit
manner through divine faith, and through the progress of philosophical and theological inquiry, now becomes—under the impulse of faith and charity—further illumined by a new union and
encounter with the divine truth as revealed and with the divine
goodness as "tasted" in and through the sacramentality of every
finite being.

This sacramentality is always present—every creature is of
itself by its nature a sign that reveals something of the presence,
truth, and goodness of God. But it is necessary that the sacramentality be *actualized*, be appreciated, known, and savored as
such, and not just in a general, purely theoretical, abstract manner, but even in the very concrete and individual instance of
knowing, loving, and dealing with each creature. That such a
continual actualization is really possible is attested by many of
the saints. Of course, there can be many degrees of such an
actualization. The fundamental determinant of this actualization
must be the intensity of the faith and charity that one brings
to such a contemplation. But the actually achieved articulation of
the vision of faith, which sees all creatures in such a relation to
God, is also a determinant of this actualization of sacramentality.
It is true that for an intense faith a minimum degree of articulation may be quite sufficient even for a relatively continual actualization of the sacramentality of creatures. But we might
expect that a far more nuanced Christian vision, one that might

be the result of successful Christian education, would be a great aid to this actualization.

Such an actualization of sacramentality certainly deserves the name of Christian contemplation in action. But it would be a mistake to understand this actualization in too narrow a sense, as if it led only to a pure "seeing" and "tasting" that would be only a prolongation of the purely "contemplative" (in the ordinary sense) aspect of our existence. In fact, this same actualization is possible in quite another direction—that of the understanding of the concrete situation in which one is and of the demands for action that this situation makes upon us. Such a concrete situation is more than a sacrament of divine truth and goodness; it is also a sacrament of the divine will for each of us, a sacrament of the immediate divine providence and governance of all things in all things. To a certain more active temperament, this aspect of contemplation in action might indeed be much more pronounced than that of the actualization of a mere sacrament of divine truth and goodness as such. But it is unnecessary here to do more than to point out the possibilities. In fact, both of these aspects of this sacramentality of creatures call for actualization in an integrally Christian contemplation in action.

The relation of such a contemplation in action to "formal prayer" is not difficult to see. If it is understood that this kind of contemplation in action wholly depends in the first place upon firm faith and an intense supernatural charity that is indeed ever seeking for God in and through all the details of life and work, and if it is further understood that immediate interpersonal communion with God through supernatural charity is the

181

principal purpose, even the whole purpose of formal prayer, then a very close relation between formal prayer and contemplation in action comes to light. It is in formal prayer that we come to greater consciousness of our union and communion with God in a fully interpersonal manner. The contribution of contemplation in action is not to produce, of itself and as such, either such an interpersonal communion or a deeper fundamental consciousness of this communion, but rather to add a certain dimension of light and taste. In contemplation in action the sign-value of every one of the works of God in men and things is allowed to impress itself upon the one who already is in an obscure loving communion with the divine presence. This sign-value is an opportunity for the one who loves God to know and taste him just a little more. Surely it is a mark of every friendship to desire to know more fully the truth, and to taste more fully the goodness, as fully as possible, of the one who is loved. Such knowledge and taste will, of course, also lead to a further degree of love—and so the cycle of loving contemplation and communion can proceed in an ever intensifying manner.

Such a mode of contemplation in action would not call for the introduction of any extraordinary principle in the ontological order, at least not for anything more extraordinary than the structure of faith, hope, and charity, interpersonal communion with God, and some degree of articulation of Christian understanding in faith (especially regarding the infinity, transcendence, and omnipresence of God). No special "mystical light" like that which is necessary for the "transforming union" need be considered. Indeed, this is a "common effect" of the life of faith and charity—which to some extent could even be approached by a man without any supernatural grace at all, though never of course to the same extent. Nor should this kind of contemplation be regarded as especially Christocentric or Trinitarian in character, except to the extent that the personal faith-context, the personal nuance in the understanding of faith itself as fundamentally Christocentric or Trinitarian, should make it so. But of course every Christian who understands his faith in a more refined way will also understand that such a contemplation of God is in fact contemplation of the Trinity and of the Word through whom all things were made. His contemplation in action is not the contemplation of a God as known only to reason but of a God who has revealed himself in a more intimate manner. In this light the sacramental value of every creature is elevated to a new and higher plane, and can lead us even into the depths of the Trinity and of the Christ in whom all things hold together.

Though we are reluctant to speak here of methods of prayer, we could add that there is even a general "method" of arriving at such a contemplation in action. Presupposed of course is a profound love of God and therefore interpersonal communion with God that is often "realized," however obscurely, in a more reflective manner in moments and periods of "formal prayer." Next must come a real understanding through faith, through meditation, through theological reflection, of the real relation of every creature to God as a sacrament of the divine presence, the divine truth, the divine goodness, and the divine will. What must also be fostered is an ever growing desire to actualize, so far as possible, this sacramentality in one's continuing communion with God in love. Such an attitude need not in any way impede ordinary action; it is rather a matter of cultivating a dominating love for the divine presence, not just as "felt" in love but even as "seen" and "tasted" through all the signs that are every creature God has made. As this dominating love for the divine presence grows, those moments and periods in which one in some manner lovingly "sees" and "tastes" something of the bottomless abyss of truth and goodness of God through these sacramental signs will become in the ordinary case both more frequent and easier to attain, by the help of grace.

We have spoken of prayer chiefly with respect to that element in it by which it goes beyond and transcends all finite forms and formulations—the element of immediate affective union and communion with God. It would, of course, be possible to dwell much longer upon the other elements: the formulations, reflections, methods, and so on. These certainly can and do in most cases play a very important part in prayer. We have singled out only the most important, the most formal element, the one towards which all else is directed—lest it should be forgotten in a preoccupation with methods and techniques, and because it is the unifying thread, the one thing necessary, that runs through every valid mode of Christian prayer.

If we have failed to take much time to point out how prayer is also directed beyond this encounter in love, towards action of every kind, we have no fear that this dimension of prayer will escape the reader. Surely the loving regard of God must also lead to reflection in this light upon activity to come and to the discernment of spirits and of the motion of the Spirit. But our aim was a very limited one—to understand in the light of faith, theology, and metaphysical analysis something of the ontological structure of some modes of contemplative prayer.

Of course, formal prayer is by no means the whole matter of union and communion with God. Such prayer is a reflective conscious encounter with God as the focus of affective regard. But it is the love here which counts above all, more than the conscious recollection at moments and periods of formal prayer. This love grows first of all through growth in humility and the diminishing of the love of self. Such a growth has many means; and mortification and abnegation—always important for everyone who seeks God—may be for many far more important than long hours of formal prayer. If our own treatment seems to ignore this wider context of prayer in spiritual life, this is not because we do not recognize it but only because we cannot say everything at once.

Finally, it seems well to add, in the light of the understanding of prayer as interpersonal communion with God, a few remarks about prayer in the midst of distraction. There are times, and for some there are long periods indeed, in which it seems impossible to achieve any measure of success in the use of the various methods, formulations, and so forth, that are ordinarily thought of as being aids to prayer. Instead of such things aiding the concentration of the mind and will upon God they rather tire and bore, and indeed are frequently unable to captivate the attention for more than a moment if that long. Persons thus troubled will say that they are simply unable to pray.

It is even very difficult for them to accept the idea that interpersonal communion with God is itself a matter of the disposition of the will, and that even in the absence of any degree of successful formal recollection at all one could nevertheless have a profound communion with God. They will say that they see nothing, understand nothing, feel nothing, and indeed hardly even seem to want anything that has to do with God—they are simply in a state of utter distraction.

Yet if there is a fundamental will to pray, then there is already in virtue of this will a state of prayer as a fundamental affective regard for God. This is so regardless of the inability of the

185

formulating intelligence and will to organize reflections, reasonings, and so forth in any determinate pattern focusing on the things of God. If the mind is filled with one distracting consideration after another, but without any departure from the fundamental will to pray, then the one thing necessary is there. So long as such distracting considerations fail to *captivate* the attention, that is, to draw the will away from the fundamental determination to be at prayer, then this person is still at prayer. It would be quite possible for an hour of genuine prayer to consist of nothing but a concatenation of distracting thoughts with only a fundamental feeling of being ill at ease—that is, a feeling that one wants something else. Such a feeling of being ill at ease with all these thoughts might in fact be nothing more than the faintest psychological residue from the initial desire to pray. It is possible to go even further: there could be genuine prayer of this kind even when the distraction is so complete that there is not even such a feeling of being ill at ease and wanting something else, when one has not even been able to muster the psychological energy to make an initial determination to pray. If one's whole pattern of living were to call for prayer at this time, and if his basic determination so to pray were not in some manner removed by contrary determinations of a conscious and somehow deliberate nature, then the fundamental determination of the will that is the very heart of prayer is still present. Such a prayer as this is unconsoling, but one must be confident that the good God is not indifferent to it. If behind the play of many thoughts about many things there lies fundamental charity that wants God above all, and even wants the recollection of God that is characteristic of prayer, then there is a person at prayer; and his prayer is heard by God.

186

VII.

SERVICE IN THE CHURCH

THE Church has many needs, and there are many ways in which to serve her. Still, in the immense fluctuating variety of the life of the Church it is possible to discover many stable patterns of need and of service. Always there are the sick; always there are the poor; always there are those who need to be taught the rudiments of the faith; always the work of preaching the faith must continue, and the performance of the liturgical acts that are at the very center of our Christian life; and we could go on for a rather long time listing these "constants" in the life of the Church, constants of both need and service, not forgetting the place of the pure contemplative. In this light it becomes easier to understand the idea of a stable religious community dedicated to some particular work or works. In this light fashionable demand for the abolition of as much structure as possible in the Church, even to the passing away of the religious communities, seems rather removed from the realities of our life.

There is also need in the Church for quite another kind of religious community, in which adaptability, mobility, and responsiveness to the current needs of the Church occupy a very

187

high place in the values of the community. And it is, of course, a fact that some communities are thus more adaptable, and so on. But it would be simply wrong to erect them into some kind of paradigm for all religious communities, as if the stable patterns of need and service had simply disappeared in the face of some kind of pure process of social change. The multiplicity of religious communities is almost scandalous to some, but it is also a testimony to the manifold needs of Christ in the Church and the response of Christians to these needs. This perspective of need and service affords to many, both inside and outside the Church, the only intelligible way in which to look at the Church's religious communities.

The life of such communities, observing the evangelical counsels and all their own rules, totally directed in structure towards God as the All for each member, is not really and fully intelligible from any perspective that is finally confined to this world. This life is essentially a life of eschatological witness, to the world to come in which God will be all in all, and to the partial realization even now of this life of communion with God under his perfect dominion. Deeper than any work to be done must be this sense of sincere witness in faith to the overwhelming presence of God-with-us and also to the expectation of he-who-is-to-come. It is this witness, more than any merely external work, however grand, that spiritual Christians expect, that holy religious give, that God requires of the religious community and its members. Indeed, the whole of the external and visible accomplishment of a religious community in the Church would only lose its greatest value if it were to be without this manifestation of witness—if it were to reveal noble devotion to noble values but not above all to be a testimony to the God who is

188

and who is to come, and who so surpasses every creature as to become our All for eternity.

But if this witness is to be a true witness, and not a false one, behind it must be the whole reality of a life of faith lived solely for God. No mere façade will be sufficient; the entire life of the religious community, in its work and witness, is at the same time a coming into ever more profound loving communion with God above all and also with one's neighbors, those within the religious community itself first of all. If this steady growth in supernatural life under the divine influence should finally be lacking, everything else is sham. Unless, behind and as a spirit informing everything else, this growth takes place, the religious —and perhaps even the community—is a failure.

It is possible, in the light of the distinctions we have already made, to speak of two general spheres of activity in the religious community. In both of these the function of Christian witness is fulfilled. And both come finally to nothing unless they are informed by the heart and soul of Christian life in communion with God. But in any event the religious community is at once both an organization for work—with its connotations of system —and also a haven or home in which one expects to find mutual help as well as direction towards growth in the Christian life of grace. The religious community simply must be both of these if it is to fulfill authentically both its role of Christian eschatological witness and its role of service in the Church. Mere organization would be only a human thing, perhaps even a pharisaical system; but the mere haven or home could itself be only a human thing too, a comfortable niche for a select few, that would leave much work undone and perhaps fail to show forth that active dimension of the charity of Christ to which the community is

189

called by way of mission in the Church. And yet the tension between these two aspects of religious community life is very great, and the problems are always with us.

This tension between the religious community as home and the religious community as organization has in all probability greatly increased in modern times. Both the tendency towards communities more geared for action in the Church and the tendency of the work itself to become more and more analogous to that of big business—in large schools, large hospitals, large institutions of every kind—have conspired to accentuate the problem by giving more and more emphasis to the aspect of organization for concrete action and by making more and more difficult the life of the community as home.

Much is to be said concerning this problem in the contemporary life of religious communities. But before giving it further attention, we may briefly note still another related area of tension. Just as in the social philosophy of the State, so here we must ask about the actual relationship of the individual person to the group, both to the group as organized for concrete work in the Church and to the group as comprising a home or haven. Would it be correct to say that the person exists for the sake of the group, either as organization or as home? Would it be correct to say that this group somehow exists for the sake of the person? Such questions are not at all new to social philosophy, but to ask them in the context of the social structures of religious communities will perhaps enable us to shed some light on some current problems that agitate personalists and anti-personalists in these communities.

The first problem, of the community as home, or center of interpersonal communion with God and with the others in the community, in the face of the community as organized and structured for work and with a focus on the job to be done, calls for rather lengthy consideration. We must admit, of course, as a first principle that the religious community is ultimately a home before it is a service-organization. Unless this community is first of all a place for quiet growth in communion with God and with one's neighbors (first of all, in the community itself), for peaceful living together in harmony and a spirit of mutual help, creating a certain zone of interior silence in the soul that opens it to more and more direction by the Spirit, and insuring opportunity and time for the careful co-discernment of the movements of interior impulses, with the superior, so as to secure more solid direction from him towards still greater growth in Christian life—unless the community is all this first of all, one can hardly expect that its work in the Church will actually give that Christian eschatological witness of which we have spoken above. Indeed, it is only to be feared that the work will not be selfless at all, and that it will create undue pressures and neurotic symptoms and bear much less fruit even at the lower level of merely human values. If it is possible for heroic sanctity to rise above such problems in any event, nevertheless the religious community must always be seeking to minimize them if it is really a place to live in the state of striving for the Christian perfection of love.

But it would be an oversimplification to move from the concept of the religious community as *home* immediately and uncritically to that of the community as *family*. While the family-analogy has some place here, it also has some serious inadequacies. The ordinary membership of such a community is principally adult, and should be treated as such—as relatively independent, responsible, and so on. Nor does the organization

191

of the religious community for some work or works to be done in the Church fit in well with the simple family-analogy. Moreover, the common life of the community, with its presupposition that each member by and large is capable of looking after himself and of performing necessary assigned tasks without further ado, assumes that one is dealing with adults. The relation of subject and superior is by no means the same as that of parent and child, and emphatically ought not to be such. This is especially so when one approaches the delicate realm of spiritual direction. To a certain extent, some of the above remarks could be qualified as regards very young members of the community in houses of formation. But even they must be slowly weaned from any idea that the religious community allows them simply to substitute one form of excessive dependence for another, originally more natural, familial dependence.

And yet, as we said above, the family-analogy is not completely without place here. It applies in a limited manner to the order of growth in spiritual life. Without our slipping into a simple parent-children analogy, we must look in the religious community for both mutual help and direction in spiritual life from the members of the community and from those in charge. The religious community as home is, of course, a material home; but it is even more a spiritual home. Apart again from the case of the house of formation for young religious, the religious community is a place for physical, intellectual, and psychological adults—but these are adults who want to grow, together, spiritually from that "spiritual childhood" in which to some extent we all remain until death. Still, all this must go on in the midst of dedication to a common purpose and work; for the community can never stop working both to sustain itself materially in the world and at the same time to serve the needs of the Church. So always the aspect of the community as home becomes inescapably entangled with its organizational aspect. And even apart from this entanglement, the family-analogy for a religious community remains feeble and tenuous enough. It might be better if it were greatly de-emphasized, especially because of its tendency to attract to religious life some by far too dependent personalities. We might even say that we have had more than our fair share of such excessive dependence.

Actually, the distinction and tension between the two aspects of life in a religious community, between the home and the work-organization, are found in many other human groupings as well, at least to some degree. If the domain of the home is that of interpersonal communion and friendship, while the domain of the structured work-organization focuses as such on objective achievement and on the cultivation of appropriately business-like attitudes, almost any reasonably contained social group with some definite *function* in society will show attraction, in varying degree, to both of these poles at once. Certainly, some such social groups show a much stronger emphasis towards the work to be done, and the complex structure necessary to achieve it. This is only right when there is question of an army unit, a factory work-force, a school faculty, and so on. Other such human groups may, on the other hand, show a characteristic or frequent emphasis in the other direction. They are not primarily organizations to get a job done but rather opportunities for the growth of human fellowship. Of this kind are many student organizations or parish societies. Nor is this in itself in any way a criticism. We need both types of social group in order to live a full human life and to make it possible for others to do likewise.

It is possible, of course, to come to a crisis in a given group, when its principal purpose appears to be subverted through attraction towards the wrong pole: a work-organization can degenerate into a mere "social club," or a society for purposes of human fellowship can become burdened by multiplying patterns of "organization for the sake of organization."

These general remarks about human social groups prompt some further comments about the special character of the religious community. Though the priority of the "home" aspect of the religious community must be safeguarded, still there ought to be a quasi-equality and balance preserved between the "home" and the "organizational" aspect of the community. The same authoritative structures frequently direct both of these aspects and must constantly move back and forth between a paternal regime, a juridical regime, and even a business-like outlook. This is scarcely an easy thing to do, and one welcomes the tendency —even in the domain of ultimate government—to split off the two domains as much as possible. But if we are considering, not future patterns of government that may eventually replace present ones, but rather the present common situation in which both domains and aspects of the life of the religious community are cared for under a single authoritative structure, we must note both the serious problems that inevitably arise and the present possibilities for minimizing them as much as possible. Proposals for amelioration will be left, however, for a later section; at present we shall only dwell on some of the problems.

The most serious problem in such a regime of religious life, in which those in the authoritative structure are constantly called upon to readjust their viewpoint in consideration of the diverse aspect of religious life that is actually the present concern—and not only those in authority but everyone else in the community as well—is that one very easily does forget just where he is. Irrelevant considerations from the wrong domain are easily introduced to justify administrative decisions that do violence to intelligence. So one man may be treated simply as a cog in the organizational machine for many years with serious injury to his personality and religious life, while the whims of another may be catered to in regard to the work-organization long after he has anything more to say of value in this domain. Disagreements about the practical matters of the organization become far too dominant in the life of the community as home, and domestic problems are allowed to influence the decision-making of the work-organization.

In the religious-school community it may be very difficult to preserve much in the way of real community life because of the problems of making and keeping a genuine intellectual community and dialogue, complicated always by the never-ending discussions and disagreements concerning administrative affairs. One might say that religious should be able to rise above any such problems, but they too are only human and prone to forget to distinguish separate domains of activity. So tensions may rise and the impression be created that something must soon break— a familiar enough phenomenon even in other school and university communities. Frequently, such difficulties are resolved through extreme tact; but the nature of the problem goes deeper in itself and seems to call for new structures that do greater justice to the distinct domains involved in the school organization and the religious community.

We could go on a long time enumerating the difficulties that arise—the religious life is no escape from difficulty! The work

195

of individuals in the organization may be greatly injured by pressures within the community; especially is this so when there is question of a more original and critical spirit that would set itself against the innate conservatism of most communities as regards their work-organization. How could one improve what has worked well, more or less, for so long? But surely it is most inadequate simply to pigeon-hole such conflict with a few remarks about enduring the cross. Yet this is, frequently enough, just what happens. And all this happens in the context of a complete confusion between the technical domain of the work and the structures it demands and the domain of the community as a place for spiritual growth. Complex human relations keep flowing into each other in many ways, and their interaction becomes hopelessly entangled.

It seems almost too much to ask of the religious superior that he alone bring order and balance out of all this, giving due weight to the various aspects of community life and keeping a clear sense of their distinction from each other. This is a continuing task for all the members of the community, even though especially of the members of the authority-structure. Under the present common conditions of unity of authoritative structure for all aspects of the life of the community, perhaps the first thing to recommend for the subjects in such a community is profound sympathy and continuing prayer for the superior. He is certainly being asked to perform an enormous, and well-nigh impossible, task frequently enough in the complexities of living and working in today's world.

In our consideration of the relationship between the religious community and its service in the Church, the tension between the community as home and the community as service-organization—with many resultant problems—represents a fundamental difficulty in religious life today. Another related fundamental difficulty must now be considered—the relation of the individual religious to the community as a group (whether as "home" or as "service-organization"). We can no longer be content with such "ascetical" formulations as that the individual religious totally subordinates himself to the good of the group. This was always wrong, but it was a frequent enough cliché in the face of hard decisions. Still, in the categories of today's social and political philosophy, such a view of the relation of the individual to the group would have to be called totalitarianism, however spiritual in intent. A more refined and adequate formulation today would have to emphasize much more those values of the person that we have already spoken of at great length.

There is much less danger that the religious community, precisely as home, will lapse into some kind of practical total subordination of the individual person to the life and good of the group, though even here continual self-examinations and renewals are always necessary, especially on the part of those in authority. Much more serious in practice is the problem in regard to the community seen as service-organization in the Church. We shall here consider this problem principally as regards the fundamental matter of assignment of members of the community to life tasks, or at least long-term tasks, in the work-organization of the community. Obviously, it would also be possible for us to approach the general problem from the point of view of the day-to-day government of this work-organization; but the nature of the difficulty should become clear enough as we contemplate it "written in large letters" in the matter of permanent and quasi-permanent assignments.

Is service in the Church by a religious community to be

conceived as simply a filling of "slots" or ready-made molds, so that the members of the community are regarded as so many pegs to be fitted into them? Or is one, without forgetting the objective needs of tasks to which the group has at least in fact a long-term commitment, to approach the placement of persons first of all in view of their personal talents, personal aspirations, personal outlook? This is a matter above all of emphasis and *a priori* approach. Obviously, many decisions will come out the same from both standpoints. But there remain fundamental differences between the two viewpoints. Differences in practical consequences will begin to appear much more evidently in regard to matters like the taking on and keeping of new and various community commitments to work—for example, the taking on of responsibility for more institutions and works. Differences should also appear in regard to the disposition of especially gifted persons, with very strong inclinations to use their special talents in the service of God in accordance with the spirit of their community.

Behind these practical differences, and underlying the two attitudes of authorities, are differing attitudes towards fundamental values of the person. We have dwelt at length on these differing attitudes earlier in the book. Briefly, we must face for ourselves the question of whether the person is finally only a part to be fitted into a larger whole or whether this person is an expansive and expanding whole destined to grow to ever new heights of human and Christian maturity and freedom of spirit, growing continually and without limit with the help of grace— all that the final communion of man with God and with other men may be reached (and granted by God) in the highest possible intensity of consciousness in knowledge and love. Does the Church, and the religious community, aim finally at some kind of limitation of human personal growth; or is it not rather a matter of looking to the highest possible fulfillment of personality.

Answers to such questions are not a matter simply of theoretical theology. One's degree of openness to the ways of grace is at stake, and it would be possible to do a good deal of harm through unenlightened direction, commands, and action here. Above all, those in authority directing the work of a religious community in the Church must continually ask themselves about these matters and whether they do not sometimes allow too great a preoccupation with the work to be done to intrude upon a delicate and prudent consideration of what their subjects can profitably do and what it is that each of them is actually called upon, in the total life-context in which he is, to do in the service of God. They must ask themselves whether a consideration of the possibilities of greater personal growth in divine life really does outweigh simple considerations of the possibilities of works to be done, in regard to the practical government of the community.

Of course, such a theoretical attitude does not do away with the concrete tension between the requirements of individual personal growth, the demands of the work to be done, and the needs of the group. Theories and ideas, however valid, are not the only consideration for the religious community in its actual life. Still, they do set definite orientations and point out directions along which to go in search of more concrete solutions.

Concretely, the problem is always finally a human problem concerning both the individual religious and those in authority in the community. A different emphasis is now required in their

199

mutual approach to the matter of individual long-term work assignments. It would be simply inadequate to attempt to resolve this matter through emphasis upon mere obedience as subordination alone. This is not the only important human value at stake here. What is needed is the much broader concept of obedience according to a human mode and not according to some mechanical rule, but this human mode being understood according to our contemporary understanding of man and of his personal dignity and responsibility.

Two components must still always enter into consideration. Each person comes to religious life and lives in it with his own personal vocation, his own grace-inspired interior attitude, approach, and response to the Spirit, that he should follow in growing freedom of spirit. But the Spirit himself manifests and specifies this personal vocation through the objective circumstances of life—among them the objective facts of jobs-to-be-done, pointed out as such by the religious authority. This latter might perhaps appear to an idealistic young religious as some kind of compromise and withdrawal from any true appreciation of personal dignity. But let him look elsewhere in the world, outside religious communities. Very little experience will reveal to him that such co-determination, both by the person himself with his own values, ambitions, and so forth, and by the environment of persons and conditions around him, is in fact the law of human life. He really expects too much; after all, he is only one of the many creatures of God.

Still, it is true that the decision itself, especially such an important decision as that concerning years, and even many years, of work and effort, ought not to come *only* from above. To draw attention to the necessary correlativity of interior call and objective command is not to justify any totalitarian or anti-personal spirit in the government of religious communities. Everything must be done so as to respect the values both of authority and of the person. We must recognize that institutions, such as religious communities, ultimately do exist for the sake of persons rather than the other way around. We must continually bear in mind the real need for cooperation between the individual (and the whole group of individuals that comprise the community) and the authority-structure of the institution in the co-discernment of the actual will of God and call of the Spirit.

Yet even after all this has been said, some misgivings may persist. Do not some individuals enter into a religious community and then seek primarily their own will, even to the point of seeking to remold the community according to their own desires? Such seems to be even an ambition openly professed by some younger members in religion.

Yet diverse religious communities do have already determined and diverse structures and purposes. A community of hospital sisters, or one of teaching priests, or again one of contemplatives, is not to be thought of simply as a group at the disposal and for the purposes of whomever might gain some kind of control. Each group has its historical mission and dedication as given facts. Supposedly, the candidate would already have some definite, at least general, idea of the framework in which he is proposing to live his life. So also, the community itself might be supposed to be exercising care in informing and examining the candidate in such matters, and in helping the candidate better to understand himself and his true inclinations. The question that must be answered is whether the community—as an ongoing group with its own history and traditions, aims and ideals—and the individual candidate really do have compatible values and aims, and whether there can be a genuine respect between them, between them not just as they might be after some idealistic change or reform but very much as they presently are. This does not mean that everything must be of one cloth. Familiarity with the actual personalities that religious groups attract makes it evident enough that this is not the case! Further, groups have adjusted, more or less, to powerful personalities in their midst many times.

Nevertheless, the principal point remains—that one aspect of the meaning of vocation to a determinate religious group is a willingness, even an eagerness, to accept its fundamental purposes and ways in the spiritual life, in community life, and in the work it has taken on. It would not be a just and due manifestation of personal independence to be constantly fighting those purposes. Personal responsibility, autonomy, and initiative appear here in the willingness of the one concerned to make his personal decision before vows freely to accept or to reject them. This is his decision and only his—but then he must follow it out one way or the other, in testimony to the high value and dignity of his free personal decision.

If these observations, concerning the need for a firm and enlightened decision by the candidate definitely to accept or to reject the community in a general way, as it determinately exists with its given mission in the Church and with its given style of life, represent an important qualification of earlier observations concerning personal vocation and a personalist approach to obedience, we must insist that they do not in any way diminish the main point, namely, the need for constant respect by the authority for the varied ways of both nature and grace in the many members of the community. No one can ever be treated as just "another member" at the disposal of the superior. There are probably very few superiors who might actually tend to treat subjects in such a manner. Still, the possibility should be noted, if only to be criticized and avoided.

The above remarks suffice to open up somewhat the second continuing problem of which we have spoken, the problem of fully adequate respect for the true dignity and responsibility of the person in the regime of obedience today, especially as it is further complicated by the pressures of the work-organization of the religious community. It is time now to speak at least briefly about counter-measures that might appear possible in the face of the serious difficulties in this domain as well as in that of the diverse functions of the religious community as home and as service-organization.

Very often, it is true, many such problems receive their concrete resolution simply through prudence, tact, gentleness, and individual forbearance on the part of both subject and superior. Still, the very points raised already should be enough to show that deeper and more general remedies are also to be sought.

One way is in the attitudes that should be present and fostered in the superior. This is not to suggest any gross deficiency in this regard in the superiors of today. Indeed, many of the points to be made here are commonplace enough. Rather, our purpose is only to emphasize the fact that there *are* remedies and ameliorations of the problems we have been describing. Above all, the superior must have and steadily deepen the sense that, after all, the individual religious is what ultimately counts in the functioning of the religious community. He must understand that this individual religious has a genuine claim on the time that ought to be given him in order that his views and his state of soul be made adequately known to the superior. The superior must understand that this claim on time and on his willingness to listen does not rest merely on some rules of the group, but on the profound newness and complexity of the problems encountered by every person on the way to God. This may entail considerable patience and even endurance in the superior in many instances. But this will be more possible in proportion to his spiritual insight into the reality that this is the place in which the most important, the most *real,* battle is fought—not in regard to the smooth functioning of the system but in regard to the life of the religious with God.

Yet even here an important qualification ought to be made. For the superior must still always take into account the great value of the external common good of the work of the community. This work is in fact ordinarily relevant to the good of many souls, for it is not *purely* external, and it does affect souls of men. This fact too must be considered by him in the allotment of his time; he must give all due attention to fostering this work. If an individual religious found it necessary to seek for so much time for himself as to upset the balance and also to interfere with the legitimate needs of others in the community for time from the superior, the superior would have to resolve the problem somehow, such as by referring him to another suitable person.

Another way of ameliorating the problems we have raised again concerns first of all the superior. If he really does preside over the whole life of the community, as home and as work-organization, as a set of individuals and as a group with a common good, then he above all has the primary responsibility to see that the various values of the community should be kept sufficiently in balance. But he should not be alone responsible; his advisors especially ought to be able to point out areas of inadequacy and the need of special efforts in one direction or another. But it should not be surprising to anyone that continual adjustments will in fact have to be made in the functioning of community life. To look for anything else would be to look for a more than human social group. That problems should continuously and repeatedly arise is just a law of human social interaction. That they should be recognized for what they are and not just passed over and ignored, is a demand especially upon those in charge. That they should be attacked with whatever means available is a large part of the reason for having administrators at all.

But it is always greatly helpful if all the members of the community, so far as possible, clearly understand the general nature of the problems we have pointed out, of the distinctions to be maintained between the diverse functions of the community, and of the roles of subject and superior in co-discerning the will of God. In the light of such understanding it will become much more possible for all to work together—by counsel and whatever other means seem appropriate—to overcome stresses that are seen to be rather inevitable accompaniments of the social structure of the religious community. Once one understands the various tendencies that interact here, he can be much more hopeful of keeping them in a due subordination in a rational political order. Certainly there should be a good deal less of simple, uncomprehending dissatisfaction, whether spoken or silent—which is, of course, to say that one should have a much happier community.

Finally, the idea of a complete separation, in many cases, of work-structure from home-structure in the religious community must be thoroughly considered, at least if we are to continue in the patterns of very large-scale apostolic enterprises. This might be achieved by having two totally distinct authority-structures in the community (as has been done in some instances), or even by incorporating the work-organization outside the religious community altogether—perhaps with effective control of this aspect being shared with those lay "cooperators" who usually come to outnumber by far the religious concerned. Frequently enough, control of the work-organization (such as a school or hospital) can simply be transferred to such a lay Catholic group, or at least mixed group, in order to free the religious community more completely from immersion and involvement in the administrative "wheels," and thus to free the community more completely for direct involvement in "personal contact" and other aspects of the very work itself (as in the school or in the hospital). Recent events give some cause for hope that such changes may be on the way in many places—though they will have to go far beyond some of the recent plans proposed for "lay trusteeship."

But even if we were to imagine a situation in which such transfers of control were achieved, and in which not only the authority-structure but all the members of the religious community understood the rather inevitable tensions arising in social groups and constantly attempted to minimize them or at least to cope with them, we would still not have reached any kind of "millennium" in social living in the religious community. Such a millennium cannot be attained in our terrestrial social life, even if one belonged to a very fervent religious community. The discouragement of false hopes should be in its own way ultimately on the side of encouragement for those who might wonder how there can be social problems even in the city of God.